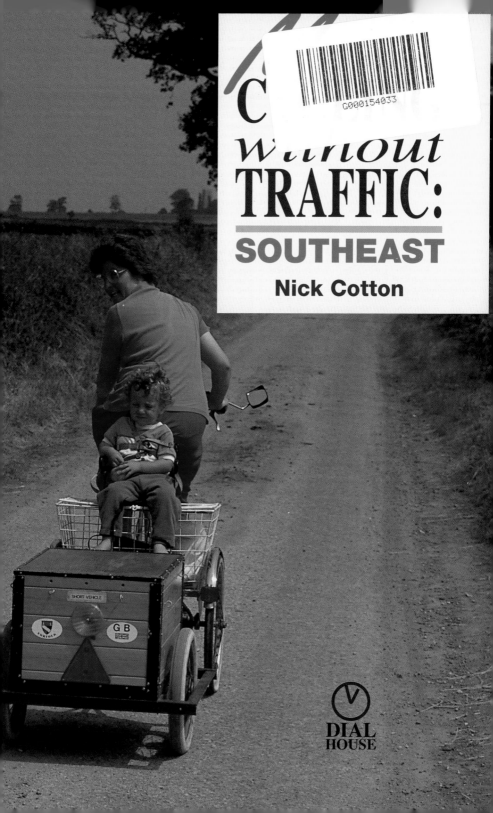

C
without
TRAFFIC:
SOUTHEAST

Nick Cotton

DIAL
HOUSE

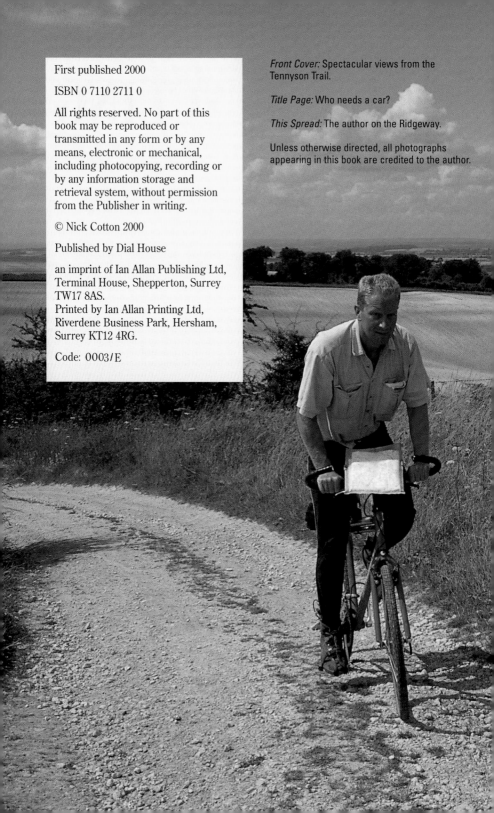

First published 2000

ISBN 0 7110 2711 0

Published by Dial House

an imprint of Ian Allan Publishing Ltd, Terminal House, Shepperton, Surrey TW17 8AS.
Printed by Ian Allan Printing Ltd, Riverdene Business Park, Hersham, Surrey KT12 4RG.

Code: 0003/E

Front Cover: Spectacular views from the Tennyson Trail.

Title Page: Who needs a car?

This Spread: The author on the Ridgeway.

Unless otherwise directed, all photographs appearing in this book are credited to the author.

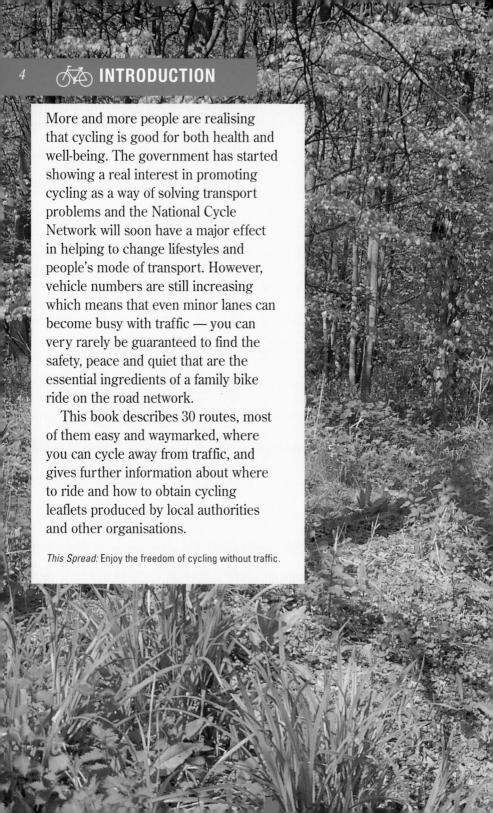

More and more people are realising that cycling is good for both health and well-being. The government has started showing a real interest in promoting cycling as a way of solving transport problems and the National Cycle Network will soon have a major effect in helping to change lifestyles and people's mode of transport. However, vehicle numbers are still increasing which means that even minor lanes can become busy with traffic — you can very rarely be guaranteed to find the safety, peace and quiet that are the essential ingredients of a family bike ride on the road network.

This book describes 30 routes, most of them easy and waymarked, where you can cycle away from traffic, and gives further information about where to ride and how to obtain cycling leaflets produced by local authorities and other organisations.

This Spread: Enjoy the freedom of cycling without traffic.

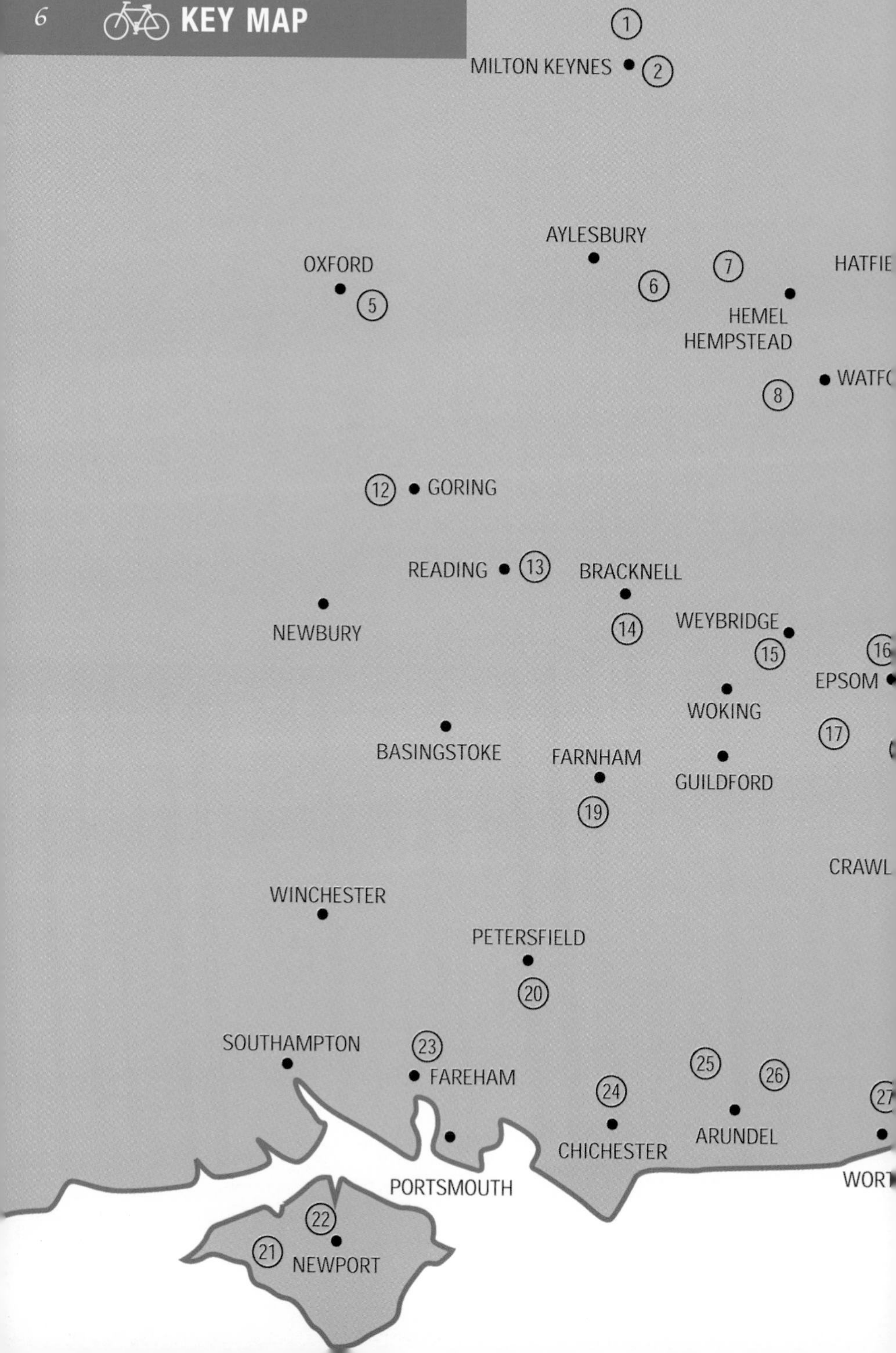

🚲 KEY MAP

①

MILTON KEYNES ● ②

AYLESBURY
●

OXFORD ⑥ ⑦ HATFIE
●
⑤ HEMEL
HEMPSTEAD ●

⑧ ● WATF(

⑫ ● GORING

READING ● ⑬ BRACKNELL

NEWBURY ⑭ WEYBRIDGE ●
● ⑮ ⑯

EPSOM ●
WOKING ●
BASINGSTOKE FARNHAM ● ⑰
● ● GUILDFORD
⑲

CRAWL

WINCHESTER
●
PETERSFIELD
●
⑳

SOUTHAMPTON ㉓
● FAREHAM ㉕ ㉖
● ㉔ ●
● ARUNDEL ㉗

CHICHESTER ●

PORTSMOUTH WOR

㉒
㉑ NEWPORT

IPSWICH

③

BISHOP'S
STORTFORD

COLCHESTER
④

HARLOW

⑨

⑪

CHELMSFORD

⑩

NDON

CANTERBURY

MAIDSTONE

㉚

TUNBRIDGE
WELLS

ASHFORD

㉙

HASTINGS

RIGHTON

The first volume of *Cycling Without Traffic: Southeast* proved to be so popular that it seemed a good idea to produce a second volume with 30 more traffic-free rides covering the southeast of the country. In the time that has elapsed between researching the first and second volumes many local authorities have produced high-quality traffic-free routes, often in conjunction with Sustrans, an engineering charity based in Bristol which was awarded £43 million by the National Lottery in 1995 to create the National Cycle Network. See below for more details.

The trails can be divided into five categories:

1. DISMANTLED RAILWAYS

The vast majority of Britain's railway system was built in the 50 years from 1830 to 1880. After the invention of the car and the development of the road network from the turn of the 20th century onwards, the railways went into decline and in the 1960s many of the lines were closed and the tracks lifted. This was the famous 'Beeching Axe'. It is a great tragedy that Dr Beeching was not a keen leisure cyclist! Had he set in motion the development of leisure cycle trails along the course of the railways he was so busy closing then we could boast one of the finest recreational cycling networks in the world.

As it is, many of the railways were sold off in small sections to adjacent landowners and the continuity of long sections of dismantled track was lost. Almost 40 years on, some local authorities have created some fine trails along the course of the dismantled railways. Within this book the Downs Link, the Newport to Cowes Cyclepath and the Centurion Way are all good examples. The first *Cycling Without Traffic: Southeast* covered other popular railway paths in the region such as the Cuckoo Trail in Sussex, the Worth Way and Forest Way near East Grinstead and the Flitch Way in Essex.

Dismantled railways make good cycle trails for two reasons. First, the gradients tend to be very gentle, and secondly, the broad stone base is ideal for the top dressing which creates a smooth firm surface for bicycles. Seven of the routes in this book use dismantled railways for all or part of the ride.

To find out what your own authority intends to do in the future about cycle trails in your area, contact the Planning Department of your county council (see pages 109-110). Alternatively, if you wish to get involved on a national level, contact Sustrans, 35 King Street, Bristol BS1 4DZ (Tel: 0117 929 0888), the organisation responsible for building the 8,000-mile National Cycle Network which will be completed in the year 2005. The Millennium Routes, covering the first 2,500 miles of the network, will be ready by the year 2000.

2. FORESTRY COMMISSION LAND

There are eight waymarked trails on Forestry Commission land:
1. Wendover Woods, northeast of Wendover (Route 6, page 38).
2. Aston Hill Woods, northeast of Wendover (mountain biking).
3. Alice Holt Forest, southwest of Farnham (Route 19, page 66).
4. West Walk, northwest of Fareham (Route 23, page 78).
5. Queen Elizabeth Country Park, south of Petersfield (Route 20, page 68).
6. Houghton Forest, northwest of Arundel (Route 25, page 84).
7. Friston Forest, west of Eastbourne (covered in the first *Cycling Without Traffic: Southeast* book).
8. Bedgebury, southwest of Cranbrook (Route 29, page 96).

Left: Dismantled railways make excellent cycle trails.

Right: Easy cycling along the course of an old railway.

As a general rule, it is permissible to cycle on the hard forestry tracks in other woodland owned by the Forestry Commission, but there are some exceptions. The chapter on the Forestry Commission (see page 106) gives details of the locations of their sites, and addresses and phone numbers of regional offices so that you can find out the exact regulations (which may change at any time due to logging operations).

The area to the south and southwest of London is particularly well blessed with woodlands appropriate for cycling: there are some 20 large holdings owned by the Forestry Commission with open access to the woodland if you stay on the hard forest roads.

3. CANAL TOWPATHS

The British Waterways Board has undertaken a national survey of its 2,000 miles of towpath to see what percentage is suitable for cycling. Unfortunately, the initial results are not very encouraging — only about 10% meet the specified requirements. In certain cases regional waterways boards have co-ordinated with local authorities and the Countryside Commission to improve the towpaths for all users. It is to be hoped that this collaboration continues and extends throughout the country.

Cycling along canal towpaths can provide plenty of interest — wildlife, barges and locks — and the gradient tends to be flat. However, even the best-quality towpaths are not places to cycle fast as they are often busy with anglers and walkers and it is rare that cycling two-abreast is feasible.

The chapter on canals (see page 104) gives you a map of the canal network in the Southeast and details of the waterways boards to contact for further information about the towpaths nearest to you.

4. RESERVOIRS

Large reservoirs can sometimes provide excellent cycling opportunities: the rides are circular, the setting is often very beautiful and there is the added attraction of waterfowl to see. Two rides around reservoirs are described in full: Alton Water, near Ipswich, and Willen Lake and Caldecotte Lake in Milton Keynes.

5. CYCLING ELSEWHERE

If you wish to venture beyond the relatively protected world of cycle trails, there are two choices: either write away for leaflets produced by local authorities describing rides on quiet lanes through the countryside (details are given on page 109), or devise your own route.

Should you choose the second course, study the relevant Ordnance Survey Landranger map: the yellow roads represent the smaller, quieter lanes. When cycling off-road, you must stay on legal rights of way. It is illegal to cycle on footpaths, but you are allowed to use bridleways, byways open to all traffic (BOATs) and roads used as public paths (RUPPs). These are all marked on Ordnance Survey maps. Devising routes 'blind' can sometimes be a bit of a hit-or-miss affair, however. Some tracks may turn out to be very muddy and overgrown, and other hazards include blocked paths, locked gates and inadequate or non-existent waymarking. If you feel strongly about the condition of a right of way, contact the Rights of Way Department of your local authority and report the problems you have found.

THE COUNTRY CODE

- Enjoy the countryside and respect its life and work.
- Guard against all risk of fire.
- Fasten all gates.
- Keep your dogs under close control.
- Keep to rights of way across farmland.
- Use gates and stiles to cross fences, hedges and walls.
- Leave livestock, crops and machinery alone.
- Take your litter home.
- Help to keep all water clean.
- Protect wildlife, plants and trees.
- Take special care on country roads.
- Make no unnecessary noise.

Left: Top grade canal towpath in the Lee Valley.

Top Right: Picnic spot in Bedgebury Forest (see page 96)

Right: Summertime and the cycling is easy.

Bicycles should be thoroughly overhauled on a regular basis but there are certain things worth checking before each ride, and knowledge of how to mend a puncture is essential.

The four most important things to check are:

1. Do both the front and rear brakes work effectively?
2. Are the tyres inflated hard?
3. Is the chain oiled?
4. Is the saddle the right height? (Low enough when sitting in the saddle to be able to touch the ground with your toes; high enough to have your leg almost straight when you are pedalling.)

Right: Always carry a basic tool kit.

Other clickings, grindings, gratings, crunchings, rattling, squeakings, wobblings and rubbings either mean that your bike needs oiling and parts need adjusting, or a trip to your local bike mechanic is long overdue. Try to give a bike shop as much warning as possible; do not expect to turn up and have your bike fixed on the spot.

MENDING A PUNCTURE

You will need:
- a spanner to undo the nuts holding the wheel to the frame.
- tyre levers to ease the tyre off the rim.
- glue and patches.
- a pump.

These items should always be carried, even on short rides, as walking with a bike with a flat tyre is not much fun.

1. Remove the wheel which has the puncture, using a spanner to undo the nuts on the hub if it is not fitted with quick-release levers. (You will probably have to unhitch the brake cable in order to remove the wheel.)

2. Remove the tyre from the rim, using tyre levers if the fit is tight. Insert two levers under the rim a few inches apart and push on them together to free the tyre from the rim, taking care not to pinch the inner tube. Work the levers around the rim until the tyre is completely free.

3. Remove the dust cap and any locking ring from the valve. Push the valve inside the tyre then gently pull the inner tube out.

4. Partially inflate the tyre and pass it close to your ear until you hear a hiss (or close to your cheek or lips to feel the escaping air). Locate the puncture and mark it with a cross, using the crayon you should have in the puncture repair kit. (It is not often that you need to use a bucket of water to locate a puncture: you can almost always hear it or feel it.)

5. Deflate the tyre, by pushing in the valve. Hold the tyre so that the section with the puncture is tight over your knuckles. If you have sandpaper in the repair kit, lightly roughen the area around the puncture.

6. Spread glue thinly over the puncture, covering an area slightly larger than the patch you are going to use. **Leave to dry for at least five minutes.** This is the stage at which many people go wrong: they try to fix the patch too soon. The glue is not an adhesive, it is actually melting the rubber.

Left: Traffic-free trails can be enjoyed by *all* the family.

Right: Always carry a pump and puncture repair kit.

7. While waiting for the glue to do its stuff, check the inside of the tyre for any obvious thorn or piece of glass which may have caused the puncture. Run your finger slowly and sensitively around the inside of the tyre to see if you can find the cause of the puncture.

8. After waiting at least five minutes for the glue, select a patch, remove the foil and push the patch firmly into the middle of the gluey area. Peel off the backing paper. If you have a lump of chalk in the repair kit, dust the area with some grated chalk.

9. Replace the tube inside the tyre, starting by pushing the valve through the hole in the rim. Ensure that the tube is completely inside the tyre, then using only your hands (ie NOT the tyre levers) gently ease the tyre back inside the rim. The last section will be the hardest; use the heel of the palms of your hands and your thumbs to roll the last part back inside the rim.

10. Re-inflate the tyre, replace the locking ring and the dust cap. Replace the wheel into the frame of the bike and do the nuts up tightly, ensuring that it is set centrally (check by spinning the wheel and seeing if it rubs against the frame) Re-attach the brakes if you have detached the cable.

BICYCLE HIRE

Some of the more popular cycling areas now have bike hire centres, notably at the large reservoirs and some of the designated Forestry Commission trails. They offer a good opportunity to test different bikes, to give a non-cyclist a chance of trying out cycling, or can save the hassle of loading up and carrying your own bikes to the start of a trail. Wherever cycle hire centres exist, they are mentioned in the route descriptions in the Essential Information section. It is a good idea to ring beforehand and book a bike, particularly on summer weekends and during the school holidays.

This Page: Bikes come in all shapes and sizes.

Comfort, freedom of movement and protection against the unexpected shower should be the three guiding factors in deciding what to wear when you go cycling. Specialist cycling clothing is by no means essential to enjoy cycling, particularly on the short and easy rides contained in this book.

Starting from the top:

HELMET AND HEADGEAR

The issue of wearing helmets often provokes controversy. Let us hope that it forever remains a matter of personal choice. A helmet does not prevent accidents from happening. Nevertheless, most serious injuries to cyclists are head injuries and helmets can reduce impact.

The case for children wearing helmets is much stronger: they are far more likely to cause damage to themselves by losing control and falling over than an adult. It may be difficult at first to avoid the strap 'pinching' when putting a helmet on a child's head. Bribery of some form or other, once the helmet is securely in place, often helps to persuade the child to see the helmet as a good thing.

In cold weather, a woolly hat or a balaclava is the most effective way of keeping warm. Twenty per cent of body heat is lost through the head.

THE UPPER BODY

It is better to have several thin layers of clothing rather than one thick sweater or coat so that you can make fine adjustments to achieve the most comfortable temperature. Zips or buttons on sleeves and the front of garments also allow you to adjust the temperature.

Try putting your arms right out in front of you — is the clothing tight over your back? If so, you should wear something a bit looser.

If you are intending to cycle regularly when it is cold, it is worth investing in good-quality thermal underwear and synthetic fleece jackets. These help perspiration to dissipate, do not hold water and dry quickly.

A small woollen scarf and gloves (together with the woolly hat mentioned above) take up very little space and enable you to cope with quite a drop in temperature.

WATERPROOFS

You are far more at risk from exposure on a wet and windy day than a cold, dry day. The biggest danger lies in getting thoroughly soaked when a strong wind is blowing. Unless you are absolutely certain that it will not rain, it is always worth packing something waterproof. A light, showerproof cagoule takes up little space. If you are buying a waterproof top specifically for cycling, buy a very bright coloured jacket with reflective strips so that you are visible when light is poor.

Below: Children should be encouraged to wear helmets.

LEGS

As with the upper body, what you should be looking for is something comfortable which does not restrict your movement. Tight, non-stretch trousers would be the worst thing to wear — uncomfortable at the knees and the hips and full of thick seams that dig in! Baggy track suit bottoms tend to get caught in the chain and can hold a lot of water if it rains. The best things to wear are leggings or tracksters that are fairly tight at the ankle. However, if you feel reluctant about looking like a ballet dancer, then a long pair of socks worn over the bottom of your trousers keeps them from getting oily or caught in the chain.

CYCLING SHORTS

If you are going to do a lot of cycling then cycling shorts should be the first piece of specialist clothing you buy. They give a lot of padding while allowing your legs to move freely.

FOOTWEAR

Almost any shoe with a reasonably flat sole is appropriate, although you should bear in mind that few of the trails are sealed with tarmac so there may well be puddles or even mud in some cases after rain. A pair of trainers or old tennis shoes are a good bet.

NB: Take care to ensure that shoe laces are tied and are not dangling where they could get caught in the chain.

WHAT TO TAKE

- Hat, scarf, gloves.
- Waterproof.
- Drink (water or squash is better than fizzy drinks).
- Snacks (fruit, dried fruit, nuts, malt loaf, oatbars).
- Tool kit (pump, puncture repair kit, small adjustable spanner, reversible screwdriver, set of Allen keys, tyre levers, chain link extractor).
- Guide book and map (map holder).
- Money.
- Camera.
- Lock.
- Lights and reflective belt (if there is the remotest possibility of being out after dusk).

You can either carry the above in a day-pack on your back or in panniers that fit on to a rack at the rear of the bike. Panniers are the best bet as they do not restrict your movement and do not make your back sweaty.

Above: Most clothing is suitable for easy rides.

Right: Drink plenty of water, particularly on hot days.

In theory there are three ways of getting to the start of a ride: cycling there from home; catching a train and cycling to your start point, or carrying the bikes on a car. If you drive, there are three ways of transporting the bikes.

INSIDE THE CAR

With quick-release skewers now fitted on many new bikes (on the saddle and wheels), it is usually easy to take bikes apart quickly and to fit them into the back of most hatchback cars. If you are carrying more than one bike inside the car you should put an old blanket between each bike to protect paintwork and delicate gear mechanisms from damage.

If you would like to carry your bike(s) inside your car and the idea of quick-release skewers appeals to you, these can normally be fitted by your local bike shop.

Bear in mind that the bikes may be wet and/or muddy when you get back to the car so carry sheets or blankets to protect the upholstery of your car.

ON TOP OF THE CAR

You can buy special roof-racks which fit on top of cars to carry bikes. On some the bikes are carried upside down, others the right way up; on others the right way up with the front wheel removed.

The advantages of this system are that the bikes are kept separate one from another (ie they do not rub against each other), you can get things out of the boot without problem and they do not obscure visibility.

The disadvantages of this system are that you need to be reasonably tall and strong to lift bikes up on to the roof, it adds considerably to fuel consumption and feels somewhat precarious in strong crosswinds.

ON THE BACK OF THE CAR

This system seems to be the most versatile and popular method. Different racks can fit almost any sort of car with the use of clips, straps and adjustable angles.

Below: Always check the straps when loading bikes onto cars.

The advantages of this system are that the rack itself folds down to a small space, the rack can be used on a variety of different cars, you do not need to be particularly tall or strong to load bikes on to the rack and fuel consumption is not as badly affected as by bikes on the top.

The disadvantages of this system are that you may well need to buy a separate, hang-on number plate and rear lighting system if the number plate, braking lights and indicators are obscured by the bikes; the bikes are pressed one against the other and may rub off paintwork; you will restrict access to the boot/hatchback.

The deluxe system fits on to the back of a towbar, has its own lighting system and keeps the bikes separate as they fit into individual grooved rails. You can buy systems which hold two, three or four bikes.

GENERAL RULES ABOUT CARRYING BIKES

■ Remove all pumps, lights, panniers, water bottles and locks from the bikes before loading them on to the racks.

■ Lengths of pipe insulation material are useful for protecting the bikes from rubbing against each other. Try to avoid having delicate parts such as gear mechanisms pushed up against the frame or spokes of the adjoining bike.

■ Tie all straps with proper knots. Bows are not good enough.

■ Use stretch rubber bungees for extra security, particularly to ensure that the bottom of the bikes is attached to the bumper if you are carrying the bikes on the back of the car.

■ If the number plate or brake lights and indicators are obscured you are legally obliged to hang a separate number plate and lights from the back of the bikes.

■ It is essential to check and double check all the fixings before setting off and to stop and check again during the course of the journey to ensure nothing has slipped or come loose.

■ If you are leaving the bikes on the car for any length of time, lock them to each other and to the rack. While on your ride, it is as well to remove the rack and to lock it inside your car.

BIKES ON TRAINS

The regulations for carrying bikes on trains seem to change each year and vary from one operator to another, one sort of train to another and according to different times of the day and different days of the week. The only advice that can possibly be given that will remain useful is to take nothing for granted and ALWAYS phone before turning up at the station, to find out charges and availability of bike space. Even then you may find that incorrect information is given out: it is always best to go to the station and talk in person to the railway station staff.

Since privatisation different companies have adopted different approaches to carrying bikes on trains. The first step is to call the central number 0345-484950 and ask if there are any restrictions on bikes on the train which you want to catch, ie how many bikes are allowed on the train, is there a charge, does the space need to be booked in advance.

Right: It's easy to make friends on a bike!

Below: You're never too young to plan a bike ride.

ALONG THE RIVER GREAT OUSE THROUGH MILTON KEYNES

For those who have not yet discovered the secret, Milton Keynes offers more miles of safe and enjoyable family cycling than any other town in the country! There is a vast network of traffic-free cycle tracks through parkland, around lakes, along canal towpaths and disused railways. It is also at a crossroads of the Sustrans National Cycle Network: Route 51 passes through Milton Keynes on its way from Oxford to Cambridge, whilst Route 6 runs south from Derby down to the River Thames at Windsor. The ride described below starts on the western fringes of the town, at the old bridge over the River Great Ouse between Old Stratford and Stony Stratford, and runs alongside the river for 4 miles on a tarmac path. You pass through a narrow tunnel beneath the Iron Trunk Aqueduct carrying the Grand Union Canal over the River Ouse then beneath the railway viaduct. At New Bradwell the route veers away from the river and joins the course of the dismantled railway through leafy cuttings as far as Newport Pagnell. With the aid of a Redway Map (see the 'Map/Leaflet' section below), it is easily possible to plan several days out exploring the network of traffic-free trails. See also Ride 2 'Around Willen and Caldecotte Lakes in Milton Keynes' for another suggested ride in the area.

BACKGROUND AND PLACES OF INTEREST

Grand Union Canal

The Grand Union or Grand Junction Canal as it was called until 1929 was built between 1793 and 1805 to link London with Birmingham. The lowest point between the two summits at Braunston and Tring was at the crossing of the River Ouse. The canal authorities decided to build the Iron Trunk Aqueduct to carry the canal over the valley and thus avoid the need to construct several locks. Watermills have probably stood by the River Ouse at Stony Stratford and Wolverton since at least Domesday.

Right: The windmill at New Bradwell.

Below: Milton Keynes has a superb cycle network.

Starting Points and Parking:
1. Old Stratford/Stony Stratford. From the roundabout at the junction of the A5, A508, and A422 to the northwest of Milton Keynes, take the exit towards Old Stratford and Stony Stratford, cross the bridge over the River Ouse then take the next right, signposted 'Stony Stratford Centre' and park near here.

2. Newport Pagnell. From the centre of Newport Pagnell follow signs for Milton Keynes North and Buckingham. Turn left at the roundabout signposted 'Willen, Bedford (A422) Wellingborough (A509)' then turn right on to The Green/Broad Street (between a car dealer's and an off-licence). Shortly turn right on to the no through road called Sheppards Close. (There is no car park.)

Distance: 7 miles one way, 14 miles return.

Map/Leaflet: Ordnance Survey Landranger Sheet 152. Far more useful is the Milton Keynes Redway Map, showing the vast network of excellent cycle lanes in the area. It costs £1.00 and is available by sending an SAE to Milton Keynes Visitor Information Centre, 890 Midsummer Boulevard, Central Milton Keynes MK9 3QA. Tel: 01908 558300.

Hills: There are no hills.

Surface: Excellent quality tracks, mainly sealed surface.

Roads and Road Crossings: There are two road crossings where extra care should be taken: the first is right at the start of the ride, near Old Stratford; the other is at the end of the riverside path in New Bradwell, crossing on to Newport Road. At the eastern end of the ride you will need to use roads if you wish to go into the centre of Newport Pagnell.

Refreshments: Lots of choice in Old Stratford at the start of the ride; pubs just off the route where the railway path crosses the Grand Union Canal (both north and south along the towpath); lots of choice in Newport Pagnell.

ROUTE INSTRUCTIONS:
1. Start from the bridge over the River Great Ouse on the road between Old Stratford and Stony Stratford (southeast of the roundabout at the junction of the A5/A508/A422). Take care crossing the road via the traffic island on to the path signposted 'Wildlife Conservation Area, Canal, New Bradwell'.

2. Go through a gate, turn left and then shortly, at an offset crossroads with a wide track/drive (there is a large red-brick house to your left), go straight ahead on to a continuation of the path. Go through a narrow tunnel beneath the Iron Trunk Aqueduct (carrying the Grand Union Canal).

3. Cross a bridge over a side stream and turn left to pass beneath the massive stone railway bridge. At a fork of tracks immediately after crossing the next bridge over a stream bear right, away from the river.

4. At the T-junction at the end of the path turn left, then at the T-junction with the road turn left then right (take care) on to Newport Road. Shortly after, turn first right signposted 'City Centre, Blue Bridge, Bradville, V6' and soon take the first left (same sign).

5. After 200yd turn first right (by the second of two small playgrounds). Pass beneath two large bridges then turn sharp left uphill signposted 'Wolverton, Stony Stratford, Blue Bridge'. At the T-junction at the top turn right signposted 'Newport Pagnell, Stantonbury, Great Linford'.

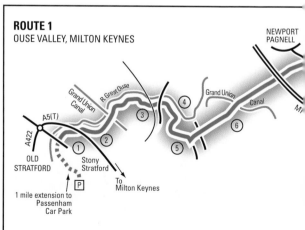

ROUTE 1
OUSE VALLEY, MILTON KEYNES

NEWPORT PAGNELL

Grand Union Canal

R. Great Ouse

A5(T)

A422

Grand Union Canal

M1

OLD STRATFORD

Stony Stratford

To Milton Keynes

1 mile extension to Passenham Car Park

6. Follow the railway path and signs for Newport Pagnell for 3½ miles*. The trail ends at Sheppards Close in Newport Pagnell.

*After 1½ miles, where the metal bridge crosses the Grand Union Canal you have the chance of exploring the Canal Broadwalk and the routes around Willen Lakes. You will also find refreshments north and south along the canal towpath.

Above: May blossom along the River Great Ouse.

AROUND WILLEN AND CALDECOTTE LAKES IN MILTON KEYNES

As mentioned in the previous ride, Milton Keynes has a tremendous amount to offer by way of safe, attractive family cycling. This ride runs along the valley formed by the River Ouzel linking Willen Lake and Caldecotte Lake, the two largest expanses of water in Milton Keynes. Willen Lake is also a major centre for watersports so you will probably see many brightly coloured sails of windsurfers and dinghies on the water. Near to Willen Lake is a Buddhist pagoda and a maze which are both well worth a visit. The ride takes you past woodland and by the willow trees lining the banks of the river. As you approach Caldecotte Lake you will see the windmill which stands on its shores. A complete circuit of the lake, with the chance of refreshment at the Caldecotte Arms pub, points you back in the right direction for your return along the river to the start at Willen Lake.

This Page: The windmill by Caldecotte Lake.

Top Right: Congestion, Milton Keynes-style.

Starting Point and Parking: The car park on the western shore of Willen Lake. Follow signs west from M1 Jct 14 or follow the A509 (H5) east from the A5 towards the M1. There are plenty of signs for Willen Lake.

Distance: 6 miles one way, 12 miles return.

Map/Leaflet: Ordnance Survey Landranger Sheet 152. Far more useful is the Milton Keynes Redway Map, showing the vast network of excellent cycle lanes in the area. It costs £1.00 and is available by sending an SAE to Milton Keynes Visitor Information Centre, 890 Midsummer Boulevard, Central Milton Keynes MK9 3QA. Tel: 01908 558300.

Hills: There are no hills.

Surface: Excellent quality tracks.

Roads and Road Crossings: There is only one road crossing, at the southern end of the ride, and this is not a busy road.

Refreshments: Café at the Willen Watersports Centre; Caldecotte Arms PH on Caldecotte Lake.

ROUTE INSTRUCTIONS:
1. From the Willen Lake car park go to the path at the water's edge and turn left. Follow the lakeside path around the edge of the lake (with the water to your right). After 1 mile, pass beneath a main road (twice).

2. Just past the Unisys building, bear left following signs for 'Milton Keynes village and the Ouzel Valley'. For the next 4 miles you are following signs for 'Riverside Walk, Walton Lake and Caldecotte'.

3. Keep the water on your left, do not cross bridges over the river. After 2½ miles, at a T-junction with a red tarmac path turn left and continue with the river still to your left.

4. At the T-junction with the road turn left then right through the car park to pick up signs for 'Caldecotte Lake'.

5. Complete a circuit of the lake — head towards the windmill then turn left and keep the water on your left. Go past the Caldecotte

Arms PH and the birdwatching point. Stay on the paths closest to the water's edge.

6. On the return follow signs for 'Simpson' and 'Riverside Walk'. Continue straight ahead past the dam at the northern end of the lake then bear left on to a broad red tarmac path parallel with the road.

7. Rejoin the outward route near the car park (mentioned in Instruction 4), cross the river on the road bridge then turn right to re-enter Ouzel Valley Park, following signs for 'Walton Lake and Woughton on the Green'.

8. Keep the river to the right and follow signs for 'Riverside Walk, Woolstones'. At the corner of Willen Lake turn left signposted 'Watersports Centre'. Follow the lakeside path back to the Willen Lake car park, keeping the water to your right.

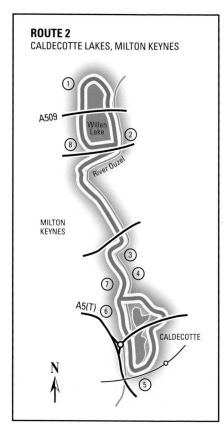

ROUTE 2
CALDECOTTE LAKES, MILTON KEYNES

Above: The Buddhist Pagoda near Willen Lake.   *Below:* Waterside housing on on Caldecotte Lake.

A CIRCUIT OF ALTON WATER, NEAR IPSWICH
(6 miles south of Ipswich)

This fine reservoir circuit is being improved a little more each year, making the route safer and easier with each improvement. Alton Water is also popular for watersports so on fine, breezy days you will catch sight of windsurfers racing each other across the lake with their bright sails skimming over the surface. Although this is a relatively easy and flat ride, you should be warned that there is a (short) hillier and rougher stretch on the north side of the lake between Birchwood car park and Lemons Bay. You may prefer to follow lanes for this section (maps showing the route plus the surrounding lanes are available from the cycle hire centre). There is a café at the Visitor Centre and lots of pubs just near the route so you could either follow the circuit close to the lake itself or make this part of a longer ride exploring some of the beautiful and quiet lanes on the Shotley Peninsula.

Starting Point and Parking: The Alton Water Visitor Centre, off the B1080 between Stutton and Holbrook, 6 miles south of Ipswich and 4 miles east of the A12 at Capel St Mary.

Distance: 8-mile circuit.

Map/Leaflet: Ordnance Survey Landranger Sheet 169 or there is an A4 leaflet available from the Visitor Centre or Cycle Hire Centre which shows the lanes in the immediate vicinity and the location of the pubs.

Hills: There are a few short hills on the north side of the lake.

Surface: Mainly good quality gravel tracks. Some short, rough sections on the north side of the lake.

Roads and Road Crossings: There is a very short on-road section, crossing the bridge at the western end of the lake.

Refreshments: Café at the Visitor Centre; White Horse PH, Tattingstone White Horse; Wheatsheaf PH, Tattingstone; King's Head PH, Stutton; The Compasses PH and the Swan Inn PH, Holbrook.

Cycle Hire: At the Visitor Centre. From spring to autumn the cycle hire centre is open every weekend, Bank Holidays and during the school holidays. In winter (November to February inclusive) it is necessary to phone in advance. Tel: 01473 328873.

ROUTE INSTRUCTIONS:
The route is well signposted.

1. From the Visitor Centre keep the water to your left and follow the trail ('Alton Water Circuit') past the sailing club, over the dam wall then turn left just before the fence.

2. Certain sections on the far side of the lake are a bit rough. At the car park and road turn left over the bridge then left again through a gate on to a gravel track, following the bike route signposts.

3. At the T-junction with tarmac turn right uphill for 150yd then left on to a gravel track parallel with the road and follow this back to the start.

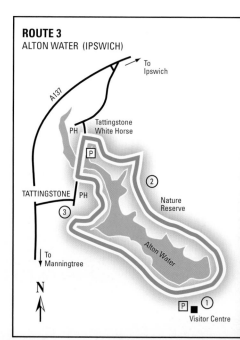

ROUTE 3
ALTON WATER (IPSWICH)

Top: Wild flowers at the edge of Alton Water.

Above: Excellent waymarking on the lakeside route.

Right: The Bristol Arms pub on the Shotley Peninsula, near Ipswich. *East of England Tourist Board Collection*

THE RIVERSIDE PATH BETWEEN COLCHESTER AND WIVENHOE

This ride links two clusters of beautiful old buildings, one in the very heart of Colchester and the other around Wivenhoe Quay, via a mixture of quiet streets, paths through parkland and (for the greater part of the ride) a traffic-free riverside path along the River Colne from the southeastern edge of Colchester past the University of Essex to Wivenhoe railway station. It is well worth going beyond the station to explore the quay and pubs by the riverside in Wivenhoe. For those of you looking for a totally traffic-free ride it would be best to start at Wivenhoe station and turn around at the end of the

cyclepath after 3 miles. However, if you are prepared to use some short sections on quiet streets you soon join another traffic-free stretch alongside the river and through parkland, arriving right in the heart of Colchester's historic city centre. As this ride is part of Sustrans' National Route 1 it is likely that the short sections on roads will be improved year by year with traffic calming and segregated cycle lanes.

BACKGROUND AND PLACES OF INTEREST

Colchester
This ancient town stands on the site of the Roman town of Camulodunum which was founded in AD50. The huge keep of the Norman castle, which was built on the base of the Roman Temple of Claudius, houses a collection of Roman antiquities.

Below: Wivenhoe Quay.
East of England Tourist Board Collection

Top: Along the Wivenhoe Trail.

Above: Traffic-free trails are a great place to learn to ride.

Starting Points and Parking: 1. The railway station car park at Wivenhoe, on the B1028, 3 miles southeast of Colchester.

2. The George Hotel, Colchester High Street. There are several car parks in the centre of Colchester (the one by Leisure World off the A133, Cowdray Avenue, is the closest) although if arriving from outside of Colchester by car it would probably be better to start at Wivenhoe.

Distance: 5 miles one way, 10 miles return from Colchester High Street to Wivenhoe.

Map/Leaflet: Ordnance Survey Landranger Sheet 168. *Cycling in Colchester* is an A2 full-colour leaflet showing all the cycle paths in Colchester plus the whole of the Colchester to Wivenhoe route. It costs 25p and is available by sending an SAE to Essex County Council, County Hall, Chelmsford CM1 1QH.

Hills: There are no hills.

Surface: Tarmac or good quality tracks.

Roads and Road Crossings: Quiet back streets are used from Colchester High Street to the riverside path through the park. Two busy roads are crossed safely via toucan crossings. The only street which may carry any traffic is Hawkins Road on the industrial estate between the two traffic-free sections. The roads near Wivenhoe Quay are very quiet.

Refreshments: Rose & Crown PH, the quayside, Wivenhoe; The Station PH, Wivenhoe; lots of choice in the centre of Colchester.

ROUTE INSTRUCTIONS:
1. From the Wivenhoe railway station car park follow the trail parallel with the railway line alongside the river.

2. The railway path ends after 3 miles at Travis Perkins timber merchants. If you wish

to continue into the centre of Colchester on a mixture of mainly traffic-free riverside paths with the occasional street section, cross the road at the toucan crossing and follow the cycle lane right then round to the left.

3. Follow Hawkins Road through the industrial estate (this is the busiest road of the urban section). At the T-junction at the end, turn left then bear right on to the cycle lane and follow this round to the right to rejoin the riverside path.

4. Follow alongside the river and past the allotments. At the traffic lights cross the road and continue alongside the river and through parkland.

5. At the T-junction of paths by metal railings turn right to cross the bridge over the river then left along the road (Sportsway). As this road swings right, turn left through parkland on to the waymarked cycle lane.

6. Exit the park, turn left uphill at the end of Middle Mill and follow this road right up to Colchester High Street.

Start from Colchester High Street:
A. From the George Hotel take the minor road away from the High Street. Follow the road round to the right then left down a red-brick road. Just after passing the park gates to the right turn right down Middle Mill, across the park then turn right along the road (Sportsway).

B. Join the cyclepath at the barrier, bear right on to the track into the park, cross the bridge then turn left, following the river. At the next road cross via the toucan crossing following 'National Cycle Network Route 1' and 'Wivenhoe Trail' signs.

C. Join an estate road, bear left then turn left over a disused bridge and right on to Hawkins Road (before the level crossing). At the end of Hawkins Road cross to the right on to the cycle facility on the pavement and follow this (via a toucan crossing) to the start of the Wivenhoe Trail. It is 3 miles to Wivenhoe railway station.

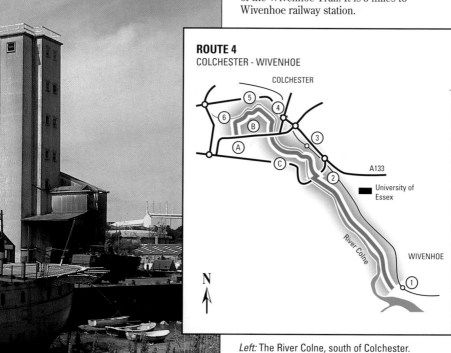

ROUTE 4
COLCHESTER - WIVENHOE

COLCHESTER

A133

University of Essex

River Colne

WIVENHOE

N

Left: The River Colne, south of Colchester.

WATERWAYS THROUGH OXFORD

Oxford has long been a city dominated by bikes and recent developments have made cycling in the city more pleasant as the use of cars in the central area has been restricted still further. This ride explores the towpaths of two of the city's waterways: the Thames on the southern half of the ride and the Oxford Canal on the northern section. The area explored by the ride lies within the ring road; north and south of the ring road the towpaths become much rougher and narrower. There are many architectural attractions along the way including the bridge at Iffley Lock and the folly at Folly Bridge. The southern half of this ride overlaps with Sustrans' National

Cycle Network which continues south via a newly-built track alongside the railway to Radley and Abingdon.
NB: This ride is also popular with walkers. Please ride with consideration for other users, let people know you are coming and thank them if they step aside for you. Where the path is narrow show courtesy by pulling in and letting walkers pass; you will be doing everyone a favour by creating goodwill between walkers and cyclists!

Oxford

The centre of the city is dominated by the famous university with its scores of magnificent colleges and libraries. Children will particularly like the gargoyles along Queen's Lane. When you have finished cycling perhaps you would like to try your hand at punting! Punts can be hired at Folly Bridge or Magdalen Bridge.

Above: The Oxford University Boat Club.

Left: The Oxford Canal through Oxford.

Starting Point and Parking: The Park & Ride car park just off the ring road at the south of Oxford (at the junction of the A4144 and the A423, to the east of the A34). Alternatively, if starting from central Oxford, the Thames towpath can be joined at Folly Bridge or the Oxford Canal towpath just west of the railway station on Botley Road.

Distance: 6 miles one way, 12 miles return.

Map/Leaflet: Ordnance Survey Landranger Sheet 164. Better still is the Oxford Cycling Map produced by CycleCity Guides (£4.95). Oxfordshire County Council and Oxford City Council have produced an excellent full-colour A2 leaflet, *Cycle into Oxford*, available from Oxford City Council, Department of Environmental Services, Clarendon House, Cornmarket Street, Oxford OX1 3HD (Tel: 01865 252405).

Hills: There are no hills

Surface: Good quality gravel tracks. The quality of the canal towpath deteriorates north of Wolvercote and the Thames towpath is much rougher south of the ring road.

Roads and Road Crossings: Care should be taken crossing St Aldates at Folly Bridge. Botley Road is crossed just west of the railway station via a toucan crossing.

Refreshments: Lots of choice in Oxford, most of it just off the route; Isis Tavern by the Thames, just north of the ring road; Head of the River PH at Folly Bridge; Waterman's Arms PH, East Street (south of the Botley Road); Plough Inn, Wolvercote.

ROUTE INSTRUCTIONS:
1. Exit the Park & Ride car park towards the bus stop and turn right along the shared-use pavement (away from Oxford). Go through the subway and at the first T-junction turn left. Go through a second subway then at the second T-junction turn right and follow the cycle track parallel with the ring road.

2. Cross a bridge over a tributary of the Thames then just before the much larger bridge over the main course of the Thames turn left downhill then left along the towpath. (Remember this point for your return.)

3. Go past the lock, the Isis Tavern and the college boathouses. At the crossroads (with the main road) by Folly Bridge go straight ahead on to a continuation of the towpath. Take care crossing this busy road.

4. Walk your bike through Osney Lock. Join East Street by the Waterman's Arms PH and continue in the same direction. As the street swings round to the left climb the steps to cross the small bridge over the stream.

5. Turn right along the pavement, walking your bike as far as the toucan crossing. Cross the main road on to Abbey Road opposite. At the end of the road turn left then right to cross a grey hump-backed metal bridge. At the end of the bridge turn right.

6. Go beneath the railway bridge, cross a road then the river and at the canal towpath turn left.

7. Follow the canal towpath for 3 miles as far as the Plough Inn in Upper Wolvercote. Retrace your route.

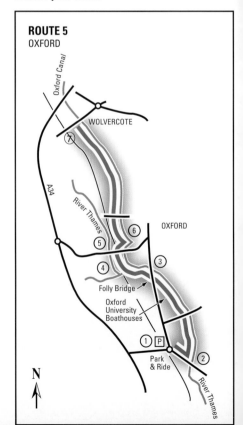

ROUTE 5
OXFORD

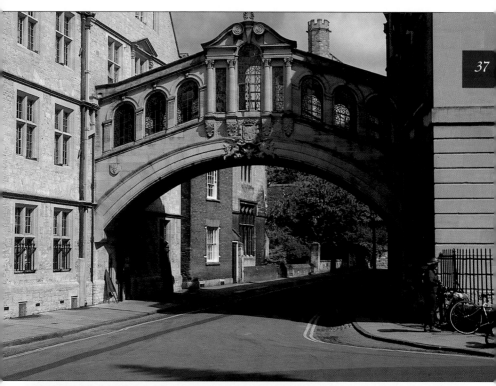

Top: Hertford College's Bridge of Sighs.

Above: Along the Thames towpath south of Oxford.

FOREST TRAILS IN WENDOVER WOODS, THE CHILTERNS

(6 miles southeast of Aylesbury)

There are very few Forestry Commission holdings of any size in the area immediately to the north and west of London. Wendover Woods are an exception and are the only woodland in the area with waymarked trails aimed at recreational family cycling. There are some wonderful views and the car park at the start of the ride is very close to the highest point of the Chilterns. The woodland is mainly broadleaf so there is a fantastic display of bluebells in the late spring and a glorious riot of colour in the autumn as the trees start to lose their leaves. The only downside to this otherwise perfect combination is that with the car park/starting point at the top of the hill, almost all the routes start off with a descent and finish with a climb back up to the car park. You have been warned!

NB: There are also plenty of testing mountain bike trails in the nearby Aston Hill Woods.

There is a Forestry Commission policy of trying to keep family cyclists and experienced mountain bikers apart so if you are super-fit and feel you have not been tested by the routes in Wendover Woods, why not try Aston Hill Woods? You will need to buy an annual permit to use Aston Hill Woods which gives you third party insurance. This costs £4 and is available from the Forestry Commission, Chiltern Forest Office, Upper Icknield Way, Aston Clinton, Aylesbury, Bucks HP22 5NF (Tel: 01296 625825).

BACKGROUND AND PLACES OF INTEREST

Wendover Woods

These woods were originally owned by the Rothschild family and were transferred to the Forestry Commission in 1939. During the Rothschild era the wood was used extensively by the family and its guests for recreational purposes — mainly shooting and horseriding. It is reported that Lord Rothschild would be driven into the woods by a team of zebras to picnic at one of his favourite spots, now known locally as 'Rothschild's Seat'.

Bottom Right: Dappled sunlight through Chiltern woodland.

Below: A rare flat section in Wendover Woods!

Starting Point and Parking: From Wendover follow the A4011 north towards Tring. After 3 miles take the first proper road to the right towards Buckland Common and Cholesbury. The entrance to the woodland is ¾ mile up this steep minor road on the right-hand side. Climb on the road through the forest for about 1 mile to the car parks/information centre at the top of the hill.

Distance: Two loops, each 3 miles.

Map/Leaflet: Ordnance Survey Landranger Sheet 165. The Forestry Commission produces an A4 full-colour leaflet called *Cycling Wendover Woods — Recommended Cycle Routes*. This is available from the Forestry Commission, Chiltern Forest Office, Upper Icknield Way, Aston Clinton, Aylesbury, Bucks HP22 5NF (Tel: 01296 625825).

Hills: Lots of hills! The car park is at the top of the hill so every ride starts with a descent and finishes with a climb.

Surface: Stone and gravel forestry tracks.

Roads and Road Crossings: None.

Refreshments: None on the route. The nearest are in Wendover.

ROUTE INSTRUCTIONS:
1. From the Wendover Woods car park continue past the Information Centre on the tarmac road towards the exit. After 200yd keep an eye out for a turning to the right by a wooden barrier marked with a green bike arrow and a 'Cyclists' sign (near the start of the orienteering course).

2. Long, gentle descent with great views to the right. At the crossroads turn right (signs will tell you where you can't go). At a second crossroads, with a wide stone forestry road at the bottom of the hill, go straight ahead steeply uphill.

3. After ½ mile go straight ahead signposted 'Short Cut'. Emerge at a tarmac road. For the short route turn right to return to the car parks by the Information Centre.

4. For the full route turn right along the road then almost immediately bear left following the 'Fitness Track' signpost. The track is also waymarked with a green bike arrow.

5. At the first fork bear right on the upper track (there is a 'No cycling' sign to the left). At the next junction, by a concrete drainage ditch, turn sharp right steeply uphill. (Halton is signposted to the left.) Emerge by the car parks near the information block and 'Chilterns Highest Point' signpost.

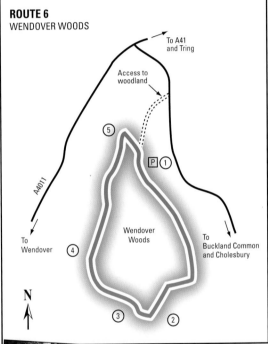

ROUTE 6
WENDOVER WOODS

A CIRCUIT IN ASHRIDGE ESTATE, THE CHILTERNS
(4 miles north of Berkhamsted)

Comprising over 1,600 hectares of woodlands, commons, downland and farmland, the Ashridge Estate runs along the main ridge of the Chilterns from Berkhamsted to Ivinghoe Beacon. The main focal point of the estate is the granite monument erected in 1832 in honour of the 3rd Duke of Bridgewater, father of inland navigation, who was nicknamed 'the Canal Duke'. The ride starts from this mighty monument (which you can climb!) and descends through broadleaf woodland on a series of bridleways marked with blue arrows. This is just one of many rides that could be devised in the estate. Be warned, however, that these are woodland tracks rather than specially built cycle trails so the going can become muddy in winter and after prolonged rain. Mountain bikes are recommended.

Starting Point and Parking: The Ashridge Estate car park by the Visitor Centre. From the A41/Berkhamsted follow the B4506 north for 3½ miles towards Ringshall and Dunstable, taking the second road to the left to the Visitor Centre.

Distance: 5-mile circuit.

Map/Leaflet: Ordnance Survey Landranger Sheet 165. A useful black and white A4 leaflet called *Ashridge Estate Cyclists' Guide* costs 50p and is available from The Visitor Services Manager, Ashridge Estate, Ringshall, Berkhamsted, Hertfordshire HP4 1LX (Tel: 01442 851227).

Hills: There is one major hill, to return to the start.

Surface: Mixed quality. Some good gravel tracks and some rougher sections which will be muddy in winter or after prolonged rain. Mountain bikes are recommended.

Roads and Road Crossings: Care should be taken on the two crossings of the B4506. A ½-mile section of the minor road to Aldbury is used on the return part of the ride.

ROUTE 7
ASHRIDGE ESTATE (TRING)

Refreshments: There is a tea kiosk open on summer weekends, next to the Visitor Centre, otherwise the nearest refreshments are either in the village of Aldbury or in Berkhamsted.

ROUTE INSTRUCTIONS:

1. Go past the Visitor Centre and straight ahead downhill on a wide track signposted with a blue arrow 'Boundary Trail'. At a fork of tracks on a fast descent bear left. Follow the main track round to the left and go past a white lodge house on your left. Continue in the same direction.

2. At the road (B4506) go straight ahead (take care). Gentle descent. Soon after passing a house to the left, turn right uphill on a broad stone track (blue arrow).

3. At the next crossroads of tracks (with a red-brick barn ahead) turn right on a broad stone track. Shortly, at the next farm, bear right, away from the stone track on to a grassy track (blue arrow).

4. Keep following blue arrows (ie not horseshoe signs). At the crossroads with the B4506 go straight ahead on to the lane opposite. (Take care on this short road section.) Go past 'Base Camp', round a sharp left-hand bend then shortly after a car parking area to the left, turn right on to a public bridleway with an 'Icknield Way' signpost.

5. Rougher section. At the T-junction with a broad gravel drive turn right then left by the white lodge house, rejoining the outward route. Climb back to the start.

Top Left: Monument to the 3rd Duke of Bridgewater.

Above: There are lots of ride options in the National Trust property.

Left: Woodland rides through the Ashbridge Estate.

THE EBURY WAY BETWEEN RICKMANSWORTH AND WEST WATFORD

This 3-mile railway path between Rickmansworth and West Watford is surprisingly green and leafy despite being situated in such a built-up area. The trail crosses the Colne, Chess and Gade rivers and if you are lucky you may even see a flash of bright blue as a kingfisher flies low over the water. The path runs parallel with, then crosses, the Grand Union Canal so it would be easy to vary the there-and-back ride along the railway by returning via the canal towpath. Indeed the Grand Union Canal could be followed for several miles in either direction, either south towards Uxbridge (and central London) or north towards Hemel Hempstead and Berkhamsted. As the year progresses the dominant features of the ride change from birdsong in spring to wildflowers and dragonflies in the summer then berries on blackthorn, hawthorn and bramble in the autumn, offering important food sources for the resident thrushes and blackbirds but also migrants such as redwings and fieldfares.

Starting Point and Parking: The most convenient car park is at Rickmansworth Aquadrome, although it is a little complicated to describe how to get there! Take the A404 out of Rickmansworth towards Northwood and London. At the Moor Lane roundabout where 'A4145/Watford Road' is signposted straight on and 'London (A404)' off to the right, complete a circuit of the roundabout and head back towards Rickmansworth — the turning for the Aquadrome is on your left (Harefield Road).

Distance: 4 miles one way, 8 miles return.

Map/Leaflet: Ordnance Survey Landranger Sheet 176. An A3 full-colour leaflet of the Ebury Way is available from The Countryside Management Service, Hertfordshire County Council, County Hall, Hertford SG13 8DN.

Hills: There are no hills.

Surface: Good quality gravel tracks.

Roads and Road Crossings: None.

Refreshments: Café near the Batchworth Lock Visitor Centre at the start of the ride.

ROUTE INSTRUCTIONS:
The route is well signposted.

1. Leave the Aquadrome car park via the vehicle entrance then shortly before the bridge turn left on to the canal towpath. Pass beneath the main road then immediately after the Batchworth Lock Visitor Centre bear left, cross a wooden bridge to the left and follow the path.

2. With a low 'drawbridge' to the right turn left then shortly turn sharp right through metal posts/barrier and car park to join the Ebury Way.

3. Follow the dismantled railway path for 3 miles. It ends at Eastbury Road post office on Hampermill Lane (A4125).

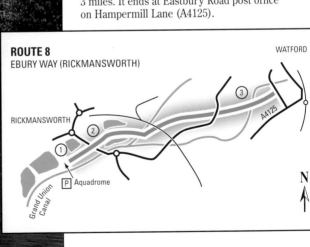

ROUTE 8
EBURY WAY (RICKMANSWORTH)

WATFORD

RICKMANSWORTH

A4125

P Aquadrome

Grand Union Canal

N

Left: Traditional canal barges moored along the towpath.

FROM HERTFORD TO HODDESDON ALONG THE LEE VALLEY

This superb open section of canal towpath is one of the best in the whole region, if not the whole country. The whole Lee Valley (or Lea Valley, both spellings are used, take your pick!) has become one of the best areas for recreational cycling to the north of London. The ride described here follows the Lee Navigation from its northern terminus in Hertford eastwards through the attractive town of Ware before taking a more southerly course through to Dobb's Weir. This is just a suggested turnaround point because there is a large waterside pub here. Perhaps you may wish to push on further and link with the circuit in the Lee Valley described in Ride 11. You may even want to carry on right into London, joining the Thames near Limehouse Basin!

Starting Point and Parking: The long-stay car park near the swimming pool on Hartham Lane, Hertford. From the centre of Hertford follow signs for the B158 (Parliament Square roundabout, The Wash, Millbridge) past the library then turn right on to Hartham Lane past Hertford Brewery to the car park.

Distance: 8 miles one way, 16 miles return from Hertford to Dobb's Weir. This is a ride which can be as short or as long as you like. The turnaround point at Dobb's Weir is no more than a suggestion.

Map: Ordnance Survey Landranger Sheet 166.

Hills: There are no hills.

Surface: Good quality gravel track.

Roads and Road Crossings: Care should be taken crossing the road in Ware — follow the signposted cycle crossing.

Refreshments: Café near the swimming pool in Hertford at the start of the ride; lots of choice in Ware; Fish & Eels PH at Dobb's Weir.

ROUTE INSTRUCTIONS:
1. From opposite the café near the playing fields follow the cyclepath running parallel with the road signposted 'Ware 2½'. Go across the recreation ground, cross the bridge and turn left along the towpath of the Lee Navigation.

2. After 2 miles, at the bridge in Ware at the end of the towpath, bear right and use the traffic islands (take care) to cross straight ahead then left to rejoin the towpath.

3. Follow this excellent towpath for a further 5 miles to the Fish & Eels PH at Dobbs Weir. This is just a suggested turnaround point — you may wish to continue down the Lee Navigation for another 20 miles or so to reach the Thames at Limehouse Basin! Or alternatively link with Route 11 — see page 48.

Right: One of the finest green corridors near to London.

Inset: The Lee Navigation offers a perfect day out for the family.

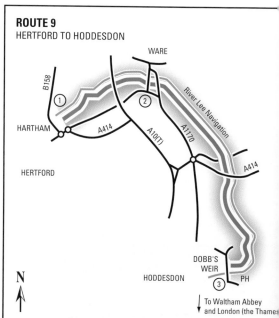

ROUTE 9
HERTFORD TO HODDESDON

WARE

B158

River Lee Navigation

HARTHAM

A414

A10(T)

A1170

HERTFORD

A414

DOBB'S WEIR

HODDESDON

PH

N

To Waltham Abbey and London (the Thames)

A CIRCUIT IN EPPING FOREST

Although there is no specifically waymarked bike trail in Epping Forest, there is such a plethora of top grade gravel tracks that it would be possible to make up any number of routes criss-crossing this ancient woodland, owned and managed by the Corporation of London. The ride starts from the King's Oak pub in the heart of the forest and wastes no time before diving into the wooded delights on a broad gravel track. There are some roads to cross during the course of the ride and of course great care should be taken on the crossings of the busier ones but in general there is good visibility at the road crossings; as long as you are prepared to wait for a clear gap in the traffic, the roads should not deter you from exploring Epping Forest's fine network of tracks. It is notoriously difficult to give woodland instructions so please do not get exasperated if you feel you are lost! The most important point is that you are outside cycling in beautiful woodland, you will never be that far from where you started and if you take a different route from the one described, it is not the end of the world, is it?

BACKGROUND AND PLACES OF INTEREST

Epping Forest
This public open space is owned and maintained by the Corporation of London. Its 6,000 acres are a mixture of ancient woodlands, heaths, bogs, ponds and grassy plains. More than half the area is a Site of Special Scientific Interest in recognition of the Forest's unique stands of old pollarded trees and their associated wildlife.

Below: Connaught Water, Epping Forest.

Starting Point and Parking: The King's Oak pub at High Beach, near the Visitor Centre in the middle of Epping Forest. This is located about 1 mile northwest of the Loughton/High Beach roundabout on the A104, the road running north from London towards the town of Epping.

Distance: 4 mile-circuit

Map/Leaflet: Ordnance Survey Landranger Sheet 167 or 177. Better still are the larger scale maps that can be purchased from the Visitor Centre at High Beach which show the trails in much greater detail.

Hills: There are several short hills, some of which are quite steep.

Surface: Good quality gravel tracks, although these may become muddy in the depths of winter or after prolonged rain.

Roads and Road Crossings: Great care should be taken crossing the roads, particularly the A104 which is crossed twice. Allow yourself time to gauge the speed of the traffic and wait for a clear gap in both directions.

Refreshments: King's Oak PH and café at the start.

ROUTE INSTRUCTIONS:

1. With your back to the King's Oak PH turn right. Immediately before joining the next road turn right through a metal barrier on to a broad gravel track.

2. Ignore two left turns (these are the wheelchair paths). Take the next left. At the crossroads with the A104 go straight ahead with great care.

3. Bear right at the next junction, descending gently then more steeply. Climb to the next road and go straight ahead (you will pass a pond to your right).

4. On a gentle downhill, take the first major wide stone track to the right. At the crossroads with the A104 take great care crossing straight ahead on to a continuation of the track. Continue straight ahead at the next crossroads with a minor road.

5. Take the next right then shortly turn right again. The gradient starts flat then climbs gently. At the final road (which has a 20mph speed limit) turn right then left. Ignore the turning to the right, rejoin the outward route, go past the wheelchair walk and at the road turn left to return to the King's Oak pub.

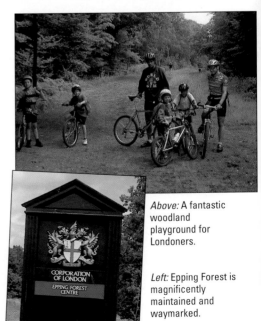

ROUTE 10
EPPING FOREST

Above: A fantastic woodland playground for Londoners.

Left: Epping Forest is magnificently maintained and waymarked.

A CIRCUIT IN THE LEE VALLEY
(North of Waltham Abbey)

The Lee Valley is becoming a focus for some of the finest recreational cycling to the north of London. It is a wide, green corridor with an abundance of water in the form of rivers, canals, ponds, lakes and reservoirs so as well as the obvious linear ride along the excellent canal towpath of the Lee & Stort Navigation

there are many possible circuits. Another positive addition will be the route developed by Sustrans down the Lee Valley corridor for the National Cycle Network, forming part of National Route 1 which will run from London to John o'Groats! The ride described is a waymarked circuit to the north of Waltham Abbey. There is a fine sense of wide, green space for somewhere so close to London. Some of the waymarking is easily missed so keep your eyes peeled and don't be surprised if you spend more time along the canal towpath than you had planned!

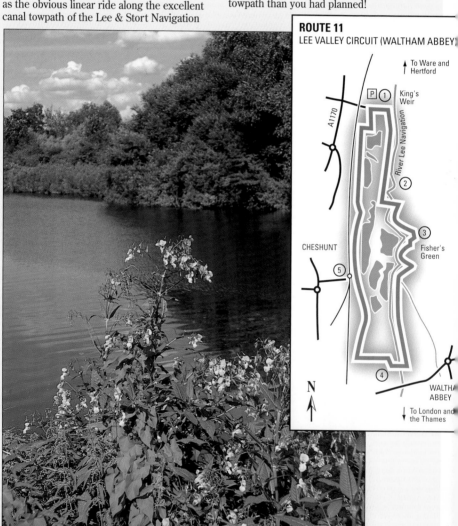

ROUTE 11
LEE VALLEY CIRCUIT (WALTHAM ABBEY)

Starting Point and Parking: There are several car parks conveniently situated for the route. The route is described starting from the car park at the northern end of the circuit, on Wharf Road (Grid Reference 373054), just to the east of the A1170 at Wormley, between Cheshunt and Hoddesdon. However, it would be just as easy to join the ride at the car park off the A121 just west of Waltham Abbey (Highbridge car park) or near Cheshunt railway station or at Fishers Green, on the east side of the valley, just off the B194.

Alternatively the route passes within 100yd of Cheshunt railway station so you could easily catch a train to the start of the ride.

Distance: 7-mile circuit.

Map/Leaflet: Ordnance Survey Landranger Sheet 166. Much more useful is the very fine full-colour leaflet produced by the Lee Valley Regional Park Authority, available free from Lee Valley Park Information Centre, Abbey Gardens, Waltham Abbey, Essex EN9 1XQ (Tel: 01992 702200).

Hills: There are no hills.

Surface: Good quality gravel tracks.

Roads and Road Crossings: None.

Refreshments: There are pubs very close to the route at Waltham Abbey and near Cheshunt railway station. Hayes Hill Farm shop and café is about ½ mile east of the route at Fishers Green. There is plenty of choice if you extend the ride by cycling north or south on the Lee Navigation towpath.

ROUTE INSTRUCTIONS:
The route is well signposted.

1. From the car park on Wharf Road join the canal towpath and turn right. Go past King's Weir Bridge and Aqueduct Lock. Cross the next bridge (a wide wooden bridge) by bearing right 50yd before the bridge signposted 'Fishers Green, Hayes Hill Farm'.

2. At the T-junction turn left. Cross the bridge over the stream and turn right on to a tarmac lane (no cars). Exit the barrier and turn right on to the road. Cross another bridge and very shortly turn right between barriers on to a gravel track waymarked with a blue and white cyclist/pedestrian circle.

3. Recross the river via a green metal Meccano bridge and turn left towards Waltham Abbey. Go diagonally across the car park to continue towards Waltham Abbey. Easy to miss! Take the third right turn by a clump of tall willows signposted 'Cheshunt 2km'.

4. Cross the bridge signposted 'Theobalds Grove' then take the next right signposted 'Bowyers Water'. At the next fork by a blue and white 'Shared use path' sign bear right. The red tarmac path joins a black tarmac lane.

5. At the T-junction with the proper 'road' turn left towards the railway line then right through the car park. Follow this track parallel with the railway line. At the T-junction shortly after Nightingale Wood turn left, signposted 'Turnford Brook car park' then turn right just before the railway bridge. Continue in the same direction towards Stipe Lane then Wharf Road car park.

Far Left: Himalayan Balsam on the banks of the Lee Navigation.

Left: Good paths for cycling are wide and well-surfaced.

ALONG THE RIDGEWAY BETWEEN STREATLEY AND EAST ILSLEY
(3 miles west of Goring/Streatley)

The Ridgeway is said to be the oldest 'road' in Europe, dating back over 5,000 years. It runs from West Kennet, near Avebury, to the Thames at Goring and in its entirety would make a good summer challenge for very fit cyclists on mountain bikes. The section chosen here gives you a taste of this ancient chalk and stone track. It is rougher than designated cycle trails and involves a steep climb at the beginning (meaning a wonderful descent on the return trip!) but if you enjoy this you will enjoy many other sections of the Ridgeway, and if you wish to go further afield, the South Downs Way is a similar long-distance chalk and stone bridleway.

NB: This trail is not suitable for touring bikes and can be very hard going in the winter when you are likely to encounter muddy sections and some very large puddles! It is best ridden on mountain bikes between mid-May and mid-October.

Starting Point and Parking: Just north of Streatley on the A417 (between Reading and Didcot) and ¼ mile beyond the A329/A417 junction, take the no through lane (Rectory Road) to the left, leading past the golf course. Follow this minor lane for 1½ miles. At the fork by Warren Farm bear right. There is parking for about 20 cars immediately after the fork, at the end of the tarmac lane.

Distance: 6½ miles one way, 13 miles return.

Map: Ordnance Survey Landranger Sheet 174.

Hills: There is a tough 300ft climb of about 1 mile at the start of the ride where you may well prefer to push your bikes. (This does mean a good finish to the ride!)

Surface: Stone, chalk and flint tracks, occasionally a bit rough. Mountain bikes recommended. The track will become muddy in winter and after prolonged rain.

Roads and Road Crossings: If you decide to go to the pubs in East Ilsley you will have about ½ mile on the Compton-East Ilsley road. This is not normally a busy road.

Refreshments: Pubs and a shop in East Ilsley. Lots of choice in Streatley/Goring.

ROUTE INSTRUCTIONS:
The Ridgeway is well signposted.

1. From the car parking area at the end of the lane by Warren Farm continue uphill on the track. There is a 300ft climb over a mile and you may well choose to walk all or parts of this first climb. It is the toughest part of the ride!

2. Fine views to the left down into Streatley Warren. Keep following Ridgeway signposts. After reaching the top there is a gentle 220ft descent over 2 miles then a second climb (shorter and less steep).

3. At the crossroads with a concrete track at the top of the second climb turn right following Ridgeway signs (remember this point for the return). After ½ mile, as the concrete track swings left into a private property, continue straight ahead on a track then shortly take the first track to the left signposted 'Public Bridleway' (leaving the Ridgeway at this point).

4. Descend gently for 1 mile. The track turns to tarmac. At the T-junction with the road (by Summerdown Stables) turn right (remember this point for the return). At the one way system dismount and bear right towards the two pubs — The Crown & Horns or The Swan.

ROUTE 12
RIDGEWAY (STREATLEY)

[Map: A34(T), ④ Inn, EAST ILSLEY, ③ ②, Ridgeway, ① A417, Warren Farm, Golf Club, GORING, STREATLEY, N]

Top Left: Typical broad chalk and flint track along the Ridgeway.

Left: The trail is well signposted throughout.

Right: Refreshment shop in East Ilsley.

ALONG THE THAMES FROM READING TO SONNING

It would be nice to think that at some time in the future there will be a path alongside the length of the River Thames wide enough and of a good enough quality to cater for cyclists and walkers alike. Sadly, at present there are few stretches of the river west of London where it is possible to ride — this section in and near Reading is one of the exceptions. Reading is where the Kennet & Avon Canal, which starts in Bath, joins the Thames, linking Bristol (via the River Avon) to London (via the Thames). It is possible to cycle along the towpath of the canal into the centre of Reading. The town is at an important junction of the Sustrans National Cycle Network — Route 4 runs through Reading on its way from London to Wales and Route 6 heads north from Reading through the Chiltern Hills to Oxford. You will see one of the attractive Sustrans Millennium Mileposts at the point where Route 4 joins the Thames. Sonning is a fine little village with a good pub and tea shop.

This Page: Along the Kennet & Avon Canal in the heart of Reading.

Starting Point and Parking: There is a car park near the Thames Valley Business Park right by the river on the east side of Reading. It lies at the very northern end of the A329(M), just off the roundabout after the A4 junction and the railway bridge. (Grid Reference 736740.)

Distance: 2 miles east to Sonning (ie 4 miles return) and 2 miles west into the centre of Reading (also 4 miles return).

Map/Leaflet: Ordnance Survey Landranger Sheet 175. A good two-colour A2 leaflet called *On Your Bike in Reading* showing all the cycle routes and facilities in Reading is available from Reading Borough Council, Civic Centre, Reading RG1 7TD (Tel: 0118 939 0376).

Hills: There are no hills.

Surface: Good quality tracks.

Roads and Road Crossings: There is a very short section on a quiet road if you go to the pub and tea shop in Sonning.

Refreshments: Bull Inn, Sonning; Jolly Angler PH and Fisherman's Cottage PH on the canal towpath as you approach Reading centre.

ROUTE INSTRUCTIONS:
1. From the car park at the western end of the A329(M) return to the Business Park road and turn left along the shared-use pavement. At the roundabout bear left through the gate on to a track. Bear right at each of the forks.

2. After 1 mile emerge at the River Thames by a Sustrans Millennium Milepost. (Remember this point for your return route.)

Left: Moored barge along the Thames near Sonning

Below: The tearoom and village shop in Sonning.

Bottom: The junction of the Thames and the canal through Reading.

3. Follow the track for 1½ miles. Just before Sonning Bridge turn right to go past the church and the Bull Inn. There is also a tea shop and small village shop in Sonning. Return to the starting point.

The riverside path and also the Kennet & Avon canal towpath can be followed for 2 miles in the other direction into the centre of Reading, as far as Caversham Bridge alongside the Thames (crossing to the north side of the river at Caversham Lock) and as far as Bridge Street along the towpath. Developments are in hand to create a safe link all the way through South Reading to rejoin the towpath at Rose Kiln Lane.

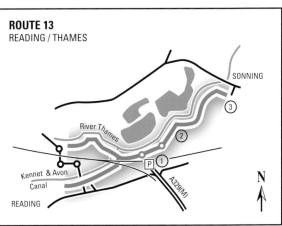

ROUTE 13
READING / THAMES

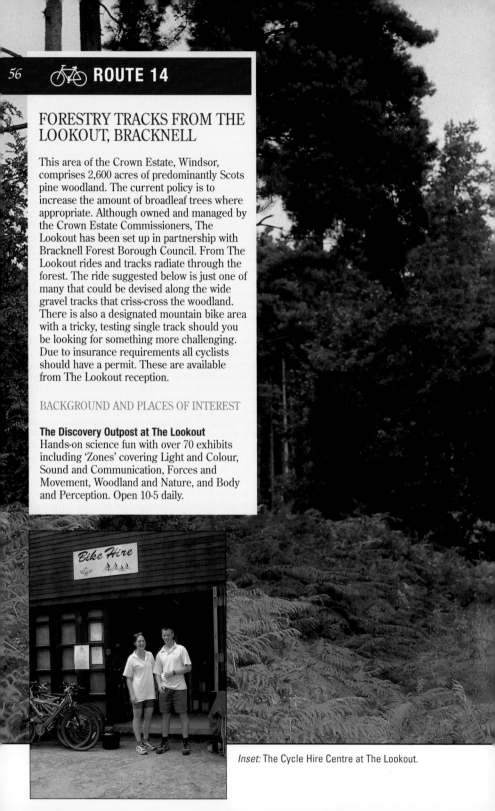

FORESTRY TRACKS FROM THE LOOKOUT, BRACKNELL

This area of the Crown Estate, Windsor, comprises 2,600 acres of predominantly Scots pine woodland. The current policy is to increase the amount of broadleaf trees where appropriate. Although owned and managed by the Crown Estate Commissioners, The Lookout has been set up in partnership with Bracknell Forest Borough Council. From The Lookout rides and tracks radiate through the forest. The ride suggested below is just one of many that could be devised along the wide gravel tracks that criss-cross the woodland. There is also a designated mountain bike area with a tricky, testing single track should you be looking for something more challenging. Due to insurance requirements all cyclists should have a permit. These are available from The Lookout reception.

BACKGROUND AND PLACES OF INTEREST

The Discovery Outpost at The Lookout
Hands-on science fun with over 70 exhibits including 'Zones' covering Light and Colour, Sound and Communication, Forces and Movement, Woodland and Nature, and Body and Perception. Open 10-5 daily.

Inset: The Cycle Hire Centre at The Lookout.

Starting Point and Parking: The Lookout is located in the woodland just to the south of Bracknell, about ¾ mile west of the roundabout at the junction of the B3430 and the A322.

Distance: 5-mile circuit.

Map/Leaflet: Ordnance Survey Landranger Sheet 175. Much more useful is the full-colour leaflet called *Walks & Trails in Windsor Forest, Bracknell* which can be purchased at the Visitor Centre or from the adjacent Bike Hire outlet.

Hills: There are several gentle hills.

Surface: Good quality gravel tracks.

Roads and Road Crossings: None.

Refreshments: Café at the Visitor Centre.

Cycle Hire: Wellington Trek, at the Visitor Centre. Tel: 01344 772797.

ROUTE INSTRUCTIONS:
1. With your back to the entrance to The Lookout Visitor Centre go diagonally right towards the Nature Trail and Walks (brown and yellow arrows), passing to the right of the coach park. Go through the gate.

2. Continue in the same direction. At Signpost Number 1 turn right signposted 'Pudding Hill'. At the crossroads by green Signpost Number 9 turn left.

3. At the junction of many tracks by Signpost Number 5 (the Upper Star Post) turn sharp right, passing to the left of the power lines.

4. At Signpost Number 6 turn left alongside the line of telegraph poles signposted 'Devil's Highway'. After a short descent and climb, turn right at Signpost Number 7.

5. At Signpost Number 8 turn right sharply back on yourself. Back at Star Post Number 6 turn left signposted 'Lookout, Pudding Hill'.

6. At Signpost Number 9 turn left signposted 'Lookout' to return to the start.

WEY NAVIGATION, SOUTH FROM WEYBRIDGE TO PYRFORD LOCK

There are several traffic-free options for escaping from southwest London along the waterways. You can follow the Thames Towpath which runs from Putney Bridge to Weybridge, then the Basingstoke Canal starts south of Weybridge and runs southwest through Woking to Odiham in Hampshire. Connecting the two and taking a more southerly course, the Wey Navigation starts in Weybridge and heads through Byfleet towards Guildford and Godalming. The southern end of the canal towpath is fairly rough but the 5-mile stretch described below is in reasonable condition and offers a chance to enjoy a ride along a green corridor through this built-up area, ending at a waterside pub at Pyrford Lock.

BACKGROUND AND PLACES OF INTEREST

The Wey Navigation

Opened in 1653, this waterway is one of the oldest in the country. It runs for 20 miles from Godalming to Weybridge and is the southernmost link in Britain's 2,000-mile canal network. Timber, coal, corn, flour and even gunpowder were regularly moved up and down the waterway. Later, in 1796, the Basingstoke Canal was dug and connected to the Wey and in 1816 the Wey & Arun Junction Canal was opened, connecting with the Wey at Stonebridge.

Right: Easy riding along the Wey Navigation.

Below: Thames Lock.

Starting Point and Parking: The riverside car park on the sharp bend on Thames Street/Walton Lane to the north of Weybridge High Street (Grid Reference 076658). You can also get here by following the minor road to the west of Walton Bridge.

Distance: 5 miles one way, 10 miles return.

Map: Ordnance Survey Landranger Sheets 176 and 187. A street atlas of Surrey would be just as useful.

Hills: There are no hills.

Surface: Stone- and gravel-based towpath.

Roads and Road Crossings: There is a very short on-road section at the start then several quiet roads to be crossed during the middle part of the ride.

Refreshments: Lincoln Arms PH, Old Crown Inn at the start; Anchor PH, Pyrford Lock.

ROUTE INSTRUCTIONS:

1. Exit the riverside car park on Walton Lane/Thames Street and bear right towards the Lincoln Arms PH. Immediately before the Old Crown Inn turn right down Church Walk (by the public conveniences).

2. At the end of the path turn right, cross the bridge and bear left, keeping an eye out for a path to the right between wire fences. Emerge at the canal, cross the bridge and turn left.

3. After ¾ mile, at the T-junction with Addlestone Road turn right then bear left to rejoin the towpath.

4. You will occasionally need to cross roads and the towpath changes sides. It is suggested you continue for 4 miles as far as the Anchor PH at Pyrford Marina then turn back to Weybridge. Beyond this point the towpath becomes rougher.

About 3 miles from the start, immediately after passing under the M25 you have the option of turning right, away from the Wey Navigation and following the Basingstoke Canal for many miles through Woking, Aldershot and Fleet to Odiham.

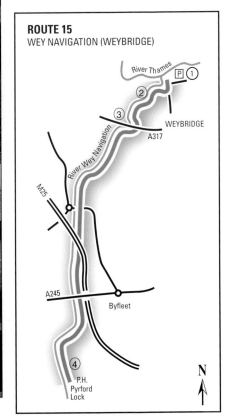

ROUTE 15
WEY NAVIGATION (WEYBRIDGE)

River Thames
P ①
②
③
WEYBRIDGE
A317
River Wey Navigation
M25
A245
Byfleet
④
P.H.
Pyrford
Lock

N

HORTON COUNTRY PARK, EPSOM

(2 miles northeast of Epsom)

This short circuit around Horton Country Park takes you past a mixture of woodland, farmland and through a golf course — as you are not crossing any fairways you should be safe from flying golf balls! Part of the route uses the course of the old Horton Light Railway, a branch line that was used to supply coal to the hospital boiler house. In springtime some of the woods are covered with a carpet of bluebells, indicating that the woodlands have grown undisturbed for many years. There is also a circuit around Epsom Common starting from the car park located on the south side of the B280 (Christ Church Road) about 2 miles to the west of Epsom.

BACKGROUND AND PLACES OF INTEREST

Epsom Common

Lying to the south of Horton Country Park, Epsom Common covers 435 acres and is a Site of Special Scientific Interest (SSSI). There are rare plants on the open grassland such as the common spotted orchid and the southern marsh orchid. The woodland area of the common consists mainly of oak and birch trees but there are also large areas of hawthorn and willow. There are a few large old oak pollards which provide homes for rare species of beetles and flies.

Above: Safe, family-friendly cycling: no cars, no worries!

Inset: An unusual sculpture near the start of the ride.

Starting Point and Parking: From the centre of Epsom follow the B280 west towards the A243. Shortly after the start of Epsom Common on your left, turn right on to Horton Lane. The entrance to Horton Country Park is about ½ mile along on the left.

Distance: Circuit of 3 miles.

Map/Leaflet: Ordnance Survey Landranger Sheet 187. Much better is the A2 full-colour *Epsom & Ewell Cycle Guide* available from Epsom & Ewell Borough Council, Planning & Engineering, Town Hall, The Parade, Epsom KT18 5BY.

Hills: There are a few very gentle hills.

Surface: Good quality gravel tracks.

Roads and Road Crossings: None.

Refreshments: None on the route, the closest are in Epsom itself.

ROUTE INSTRUCTIONS:
1. Exit the car park and turn left to go past the Equestrian Centre. Go straight ahead, following bike route signs. Easy to miss! On a gentle descent on this broad stone track take the next broad track to the right. (Bike sign.)

2. Easy to miss! Ignore two right turns. At a fork of tracks, shortly after passing a 'Footpath to Castle Hill' sign to the left, bear right for a circuit of the park (the white arrow points left but this track just leads to the road).

3. Pass through the golf course with fairways to right and left, ignoring turnings to the left. At the T-junction with a low wooden bench ahead, turn left to return to the Equestrian Centre and the car park.

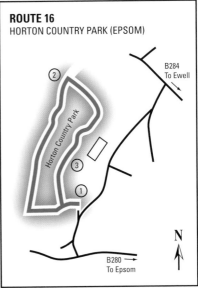

ROUTE 16
HORTON COUNTRY PARK (EPSOM)

Above: "How far to the ice-cream van?"

Left: There is an easy 3-mile circuit in Horton Park.

ROUTE 17
NORBURY PARK (LEATHERHEAD)

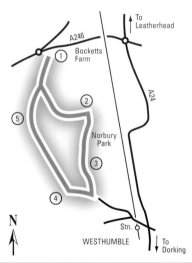

Above: View down into the Mole Valley from Norbury Park.

Right: There are many miles of bridleways around the park.

NORBURY PARK, LEATHERHEAD
(2 miles southeast of Leatherhead)

As with Horton Park (described in Route 16), which lies to the north of Leatherhead, Norbury Park offers family cyclists a short waymarked circuit in amongst woodland and farmland which seem a million miles away from the busy roads in this densely populated part of Surrey. There is a good network of bridleways stretching away to the southeast through Polesden Lacey and Ranmore Common along the line of the North Downs towards Shere and Gomshall, so with the aid of an Ordnance Survey map you could easily devise your own off-road routes through the woodland.

BACKGROUND AND PLACES OF INTEREST

Norbury Park
Norbury Park was the first area of countryside that Surrey County Council purchased in the 1930s to protect it from development. Lying within the Surrey Hills Area of Outstanding Natural Beauty and covering 1,300 acres, Norbury Park is made up of an attractive mix of woodland, farms and grassland. Much of the park lies on chalk and flint with a clay cap on higher ground. These soil types support different woodland communities. Beech, yew, ash and cherry are classic chalk area trees whereas clay supports oak and chestnut. Some of the yews are up to 2,000 years old. The Manor of Norbury Park was referred to in the 1086 Domesday Book. The present house was built in 1774.

Starting Point and Parking: The car park is located off the roundabout lying to the southeast of Leatherhead at the junction of the A246 and B2122, signposted 'Bocketts Farm. Norbury Country Park' (Grid Reference 152249).

Distance: Circuit of 4 miles.

Map: Ordnance Survey Landranger Sheet 187.

Hills: There are several gentle hills.

Surface: Good quality gravel and stone tracks.

Roads and Road Crossings: There is a short section on a minor no through lane where you are highly unlikely to see any traffic.

Refreshments: None en route, the closest are in Leatherhead or Great Bookham.

ROUTE INSTRUCTIONS:
1. Exit the car park, turn sharp right on the tarmac lane leading directly away from the main road. At the major crossroads of stone tracks by a four-way signpost go straight ahead signposted 'Westhumble'.

2. At the first major fork of stone tracks bear left then at the second fork by a large triangle of grass planted with trees bear right (both forks have a bike route waymark). Follow this track through a barrier with a sign 'Backroad to Westhumble'.

3. Go past the viewpoint. Easy to miss! On the descent keep an eye out for a bike route signpost directing you on to a track bearing uphill to the right.

4. Climb then descend. At the end of Crabtree car park turn right uphill on tarmac. Immediately after a tall flint wall to the right, bear right on to track.

5. Long, fine descent. At the next major fork bear right staying close to the woodland to the right. Follow this track past a red-brick farm (Roaring House Farm) then at the next crossroads turn left signposted 'Fetcham, car park' and follow the outward route back to the start.

Above: Woodland sunlight in Norbury Park.

THE NORTH DOWNS WAY FROM REIGATE HILL
(2 miles north of Reigate)

The chalk slopes of the North Downs, which stretch from Farnham in Surrey to the famous white cliffs of Dover, offer some fine off-road riding. Unlike the South Downs Way, which has bridleway status along its entire length (meaning that you have a right to ride along it), the North Downs Way is a mixture of byway, bridleway and footpath and you are not allowed to ride on footpaths. This section runs along a bridleway section high up on the North Downs escarpment with fantastic views down to the wide valley of the River Mole. There are plenty more bridleways nearby criss-crossing Walton Heath, Banstead Heath, Headley Heath and Mickleham Downs.

BACKGROUND AND PLACES OF INTEREST

Reigate Hill
Reigate, Colley and Juniper Hills lie on the scarp slope of the North Downs and were acquired between 1912 and 1955. The North Downs Way passes through them. The chalk grasslands provide an ideal habitat for a whole range of insects such as the Chalkhill Blue butterfly and the day-flying Burnet moth. The monument was presented to the Corporation of the Borough of Reigate for the benefit of the public by Lt-Col Robert William Inglis in 1909.

Starting Point and Parking: The car park at the top of Reigate Hill signposted from the M25, Jct 8. Take the A217 south towards Reigate then shortly turn off left for the car park (Grid Reference 264524).

Distance: 3 miles one way, 6 miles return.

Map: Ordnance Survey Landranger Sheet 187.

Hills: Gently undulating. Beyond the suggested turnaround point the track descends and climbs more steeply.

Surface: Chalk and gravel tracks, possibly muddy in winter or after prolonged rain.

Roads and Road Crossings: A very short section of public road is used, serving a few houses.

Refreshments: There is a café at the car park.

ROUTE INSTRUCTIONS:
1. From the car park go past the wooden buildings (toilets/café), cross the bridge and climb gently on a broad stone track. At a crossroads with tarmac go straight ahead signposted 'North Downs Way'.

2. Continue in the same direction past the round 'temple' with pillars. At the T-junction with the road turn left signposted 'North Downs Way' then shortly, with Mole Place ahead, turn right alongside a fence signposted 'Public Bridleway'.

3. It is suggested that you continue as far as the next wide open view then return. If you wish to go on, the track drops steeply and becomes a little rougher. There are several circuits possible if you continue as far as the B2032, cross the M25 then return via Walton Heath, Mogador and Margery Wood. (You will need an Ordnance Survey map to plan your route.)

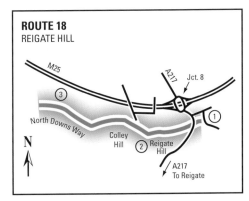

Centre, Top: The monument on Reigate Hill.

Centre, Bottom: The Sunday morning chain gang.

Above: The broad open tracks in Alice Holt Forest.

ALICE HOLT WOODLAND PARK, FARNHAM

(3 miles southwest of Farnham in Surrey)

An excellently signposted, totally traffic-free route around the gently undulating mixed broadleaf and conifer woodlands in Alice Holt Woodland Park to the southwest of Farnham. There is a good cycle hire centre offering a variety of bikes and trailers. This ride could easily be combined with a visit to Birdworld which lies less than a mile away and has a fantastic collection of birds from all over the world.

BACKGROUND AND PLACES OF INTEREST

History of the Forest
Important potteries were developed in Alice Holt in Roman times as a result of the proximity of local resources: clay for the pots, heathland turf for the kilns and forest timber for the fuel. You can see a reconstructed pottery kiln in Goose Green Inclosure. Many hundreds of years later the forest was owned by Aelfsige, Bishop of Winchester, and it is thought to be named after him: the Old English name of Aelfsige's Holt became Alice Holt.

From the Middle Ages onwards, timber was the woodland's most prized resource, the trees being used to build ships for Britain's navy. Hundreds of mature oaks were needed to build a single ship and the forest was periodically stripped of its large trees to supply the naval shipyards dotted along the south coast. More recently, Alice Holt oak has been used to build a replica of Shakespeare's Globe Theatre in London.

Bottom Left: The Visitor Centre.

Bottom Centre: The trail is superbly signposted.

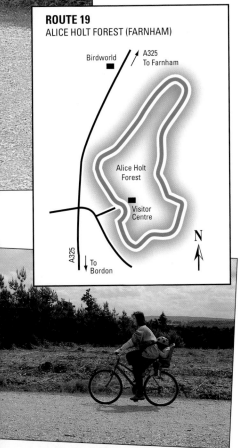

ROUTE 19
ALICE HOLT FOREST (FARNHAM)

Birdworld

A325
To Farnham

Alice Holt Forest

Visitor Centre

A325

To Bordon

N

Starting Point and Parking: Alice Holt Visitor Centre is just off the A325 Farnham-Petersfield road, 4 miles southwest of Farnham.

Distance: A 4-mile circuit.

Map/Leaflet: Ordnance Survey Landranger Sheet 186 or there is a leaflet produced by the Forestry Commission, available from Forest Enterprise, South Downs District Office, Bucks Horn Oak, Farnham, Surrey GU10 4LS (Tel: 01420 23666).

Hills: There are several gentle hills.

Surface: Good quality gravel tracks all the way round.

Roads and Road Crossings: There are no road crossings.

Refreshments: The shop/Visitor Centre sells drinks and ice creams.

Cycle Hire: At the Visitor Centre (Tel: 01420 476612).

ROUTE INSTRUCTIONS:
The route is well signposted from the cycle hire centre in both directions.

Left: Open views from a highpoint along the trail.

QUEEN ELIZABETH COUNTRY PARK, PETERSFIELD
(4 miles southwest of Petersfield)

Queen Elizabeth Country Park is certainly not flat but there is an excellent waymarked traffic-free circuit and plenty of other attractions in the park and at the Visitor Centre. For the more adventurous there is a technically challenging mountain bike circuit. There are also trails leading off out of the park on to the network of bridleways and lanes that criss-cross the South Downs, the great chalk ridge stretching from Winchester to Eastbourne.
NB: Children should be supervised closely on the downhill sections as it is possible to pick up a lot of speed quite quickly!

BACKGROUND AND PLACES OF INTEREST
Queen Elizabeth Country Park
The park is part of the landscape of the South Downs and is in an Area of Outstanding Natural Beauty. It covers 1,400 acres and is dominated by the three hills of Butser, War Down and Holt Down, which provide a contrast between the dramatic downland and beautiful woodland. With 38 species of butterfly and 12 species of wild orchid, it is a naturalist's paradise, a large area of which is designated as a Site of Special Scientific Interest. The many Roman and Iron Age sites in the park are also preserved as Scheduled Ancient Monuments.

Starting Point and Parking: Queen Elizabeth Country Park is well signposted off the A3 to the southwest of Petersfield (on the way to Portsmouth). There is a Pay & Display car park by the Visitor Centre.

Distance: There are two waymarked trails:
1. The purple-topped posts waymark a 3.7-mile circuit, with hills, but suitable for all.
2. The orange-topped posts waymark a 3.1-mile advanced mountain bike trail for experienced riders with good technical skills. There are also routes waymarked with a blue arrow/white bicycle. These go out of the park into the surrounding countryside and

occasionally use roads. For further details ask in the Visitor Centre for the Off-road Cycle Trail Pack.

Map/Leaflet: Ordnance Survey Landranger Sheet 197. Much better is the excellent A2 full-colour *Queen Elizabeth Country Park Trails Guide* leaflet produced by Hampshire County Council/Forest Enterprise and available from: Queen Elizabeth Country Park, Gravel Hill, Horndean, Waterlooville, Hampshire PO8 0QE (Tel: 01705 595040).

Hills: There is one major hill (over 400ft of climbing), parts of which you may well choose to walk.

Surface: Good quality gravel tracks.

Roads and Road Crossings: None

Refreshments: Café at the Visitor Centre.

ROUTE INSTRUCTIONS:
The routes are well signposted. The trails start from the corner of the car park to the left of the Visitor Centre by a large colourful wooden signpost (or alternatively go through the first car park and on to the Gravel Hill car park). In general terms the purple (easier) route climbs steadily for the first half of the route and descends for the second half.

Right: A vast beech cathedral in the heart of Queen Elizabeth Park.

Below: Well-graded track through woodland.

ROUTE 20
QUEEN ELIZABETH COUNTRY PARK
(PETERSFIELD)

A3(T)
To Petersfield

South Downs Way

Queen
Elizabeth
Country
Park

Visitor
Centre

A3(T)

To
Portsmouth

N

69

TENNYSON TRAIL
(2 miles south of Yarmouth in the west of the Isle of Wight)

This is without doubt one of the finest chalk ridges in the country, equal to anything along the Ridgeway or South Downs and in many ways better in that the views from high up on the island enable you to see far out to sea, ahead to the far end of the island and north across the Solent to Hampshire.

Starting from the charms of Freshwater Bay you are faced with a very steep climb, parts of which you may well wish to walk. Beyond the golf clubhouse the views just get better and better and there are a succession of thrilling grassy descents and steep climbs to regain height. At the edge of Brighstone Forest you have a choice of continuing along the Tennyson Trail into Newport or of following the more open chalk ridge along the Worsley Trail. In either case, there are plenty of hills and thrills to look forward to on your return to Freshwater Bay.

BACKGROUND AND PLACES OF INTEREST

Carisbrooke Castle
This dramatic Norman and Tudor castle stands on a ridge above Newport. There are magnificent views from the keep where Charles I was imprisoned shortly before his execution in 1649.

This Page: Guess the direction of the prevailing wind!

Inset: The Isle of Wight has a fine selection of Bridleways.

Starting Point and Parking: The main car park in Freshwater Bay, on the west side of the island, 3 miles south of Yarmouth.

Distance: 6 miles from Freshwater Bay to the far end of Brighstone Forest (ie 12 miles return). From this point it is a further 5 miles along the Tennyson Trail to Carisbrooke at the western edge of Newport or 2 miles along the Worsley Trail to the B3323 and a chance of refreshment in Shorwell.

Map/Leaflet: Ordnance Survey Landranger Sheet 196 or Outdoor Leisure Sheet 29. There is an excellent set of leaflets produced by Isle of Wight Council called *Byways & Bridleways by Mountain Bike.* For further details contact Isle of Wight Council, Highways and Transportation, County Hall, Newport, Isle of Wight PO30 1UD (Tel: 01983 821000).

Hills: There are several hills, some of them steep. This ride is not suitable for very young children or the very unfit! Try the Newport-Cowes railway path instead!

Surface: Chalk, stone and grass tracks, likely to be muddy in winter and after prolonged rain. Mountain bikes recommended.

Roads and Road Crossings: The A3055 from Freshwater Bay can be avoided by using the pavement. There are two roads to cross, neither is very busy.

Refreshments: Lots of choice in Freshwater Bay, pubs in Carisbrooke if you choose to follow the Tennyson Trail towards Newport and pubs in Shorwell if you follow the Worsley Trail (this will involve a short road section on the B3323).

ROUTE INSTRUCTIONS:
1. Facing the sea in Freshwater Bay turn left uphill on the A3055, climbing steeply. (Push your bike along the pavement.) Take the second left on to Southdown Road signposted 'Freshwater Bay Golf Club' then first right signposted 'Tennyson Way' to pass straight through the golf club.

2. Climb with ever better views behind you. Descend. At the road go straight ahead on to a tougher climb.

3. Fine, grassy descent. At the next road turn right then left.

4. Towards the top of the third climb you have a choice:
(a) follow the Tennyson Trail, bearing left into the woodland on a broad stone track signposted 'Old Highway, Tennyson Trail,

Right: The island excels at waymarking its trails.

Below: Typical chalk and flint track along the Tennyson trail.

ROUTE 21
TENNYSON TRAIL (ISLE OF WIGHT)

FRESHWATER BAY
①

Compton Bay

②

③

④

Brighstone Forest

Optional ext on Tennyso to Carisb

Optional exten to Shorwel

N
↑

Carisbrooke'. Once out of the woodland the track becomes a bit rougher then more enclosed. Follow for 5 miles, emerging opposite the lion-topped brick wall of Park House. Turn left downhill then right for the Waverley PH.

(b) continue straight ahead on the Worsley Trail for 2 miles, enjoying the open views to the right. It is suggested you go as far as the B3323 then turn right for ¾ mile to the pub in Shorwell before retracing your route.

(c) do neither of the above but turn around at this point and go back to Freshwater Bay.

THE NEWPORT TO COWES CYCLE TRAIL ON THE ISLE OF WIGHT

The Isle of Wight is a great place to explore by bike and as taking a car on the ferry is so expensive it is well worth leaving the car on the mainland and catching the ferry with just your bike(s). In this way you will also avoid adding to the vehicle traffic on the island. The previous ride (Route 21) describes the Tennyson Trail, a fairly tough challenge along a broad chalk track in the west of the island; by contrast, this ride from Cowes to Newport

is the longest and the best known of the four railway paths on the Isle of Wight. The three others run from Freshwater to Yarmouth, from Shanklin to Wroxall and south from Newport to Blackwater. The Cowes-Newport Cycleway runs for 4 miles alongside the River Medina, a wide expanse of water with hundreds of moored yachts. Cowes is of course a famous yachting centre and during Cowes Week the whole of the Solent is filled with bright sails.

This Page: Looking across towards the Needles.

Inset: Yachts moored in the River Medina near Cowes.

Starting Points: 1. The Guildhall/ Clocktower in the centre of Newport. Follow cycleway signs (see 'Route Instructions:' below.

2. The ferry terminal on the west side of the River Medina in Cowes. From the ferry terminal take the first left and keep following 'Cowes-Newport Cycleway' signs.

Distance: 4 miles one way, 8 miles return.

Map: Ordnance Survey Landranger Sheet 196.

Hills: There are no hills.

Surface: Good quality tarmac or gravel track.

Roads and Road Crossings: Quiet streets from the centre of Newport. One minor road crossing. You will need to use roads if you want to go into the centre of Cowes.

Refreshments: Lots of choice in both Newport and Cowes.

ROUTE INSTRUCTIONS:
The route is signposted from the centre of Newport on quiet roads to the start of the railway path.

1. From the Guildhall/Clocktower in the centre of Newport turn along Quay Street. Follow round a sharp left-hand bend then turn second right on to Little London, signposted 'Cowes Bike Route'.

2. Follow this road around a left-hand bend. At the T-junction at the end of Hurstake Road turn right signposted 'Cowes'. Continue straight ahead at the roundabout on to Manners View, passing a large Royal Mail building.

3. Join the trail proper and follow for 4 miles alongside the River Medina.

4. The trail ends in Cowes at the Medina Court Industrial Estate, Arctic Road. To continue into the centre of Cowes, at the roundabout by Bernard Road turn left signposted 'Cowes Town Centre' and keep following 'Town Centre' signs.

ROUTE 22
NEWPORT - COWES (ISLE OF WIGHT)

COWES

River Medina

④

③

②

①
NEWPORT

N

Above: Summertime in nearby Ryd

Right: Cruisin Cowes.

WEST WALK, WICKHAM, HAMPSHIRE

(5 miles north of Fareham)

West Walk is the largest remaining fragment of the former Royal Forest of Bere, which in ancient times used to stretch for over 30 miles from the River Test in the west to Rowland's Castle in the east. The ride described below is a waymarked 3-mile woodland circuit in this 350-hectare forest situated to the north of Fareham. There is also a waymarked mountain biking route with more technical sections (starting on the other side of the road from the car park). The Family Route runs very close to the Meon Valley Trail, a railway path running from Wickham to West Meon, so it would be easy to link the two for a much longer ride.

BACKGROUND AND PLACES OF INTEREST

The Forest of Bere

The Saxon Kings used the forest for hunting long before the Normans made Bere a royal forest. The last monarch to hunt here was Charles I in 1628. Like other royal forests, its main purpose was to provide hunting but it soon became important for timber. By the 17th century, timber was fast disappearing. To take an example, in 1653, in just three days, 500 trees were felled to repair ships damaged in skirmishes with the Dutch. Only 3% of its timber remained and the land area had been reduced to 25 square miles. Bere suffered from its proximity to the shipbuilding industry and land-hungry farmers. The woodland was eventually taken over by the Forestry Commission in 1919. Much of the old oak remains, protected by a management plan for the next 200 years!

Above: Easy forest trails are a great place to learn to cycle.

Above right, Inset: Great exercise, fresh air, forest smells - who needs more?

Starting Point and Parking: West Walk lies 5 miles north of Fareham, Hampshire. The start is from the Forest Enterprise car park on the minor road connecting the B2177 east of Wickham with Newtown and Soberton Heath (Grid Reference 597123).

Distance: 3-mile circuit.

Map/Leaflet: Ordnance Survey Landranger Sheet 196. A full-colour A3 leaflet called *The Forest of Bere* is available from Forest Enterprise, Downs & Chilterns Forest District Office, Bucks Horn Oak, Farnham, Surrey GU10 4LS (Tel: 01420 23666).

Hills: There are several gentle hills.

Surface: Good quality gravel tracks.

Roads and Road Crossings: Care should be taken crossing the minor road between the two loops.

Refreshments: None en route. The nearest are pubs in Soberton Heath and North Boarhunt or plenty of choice in Wickham.

Above: Foxgloves in the forest.

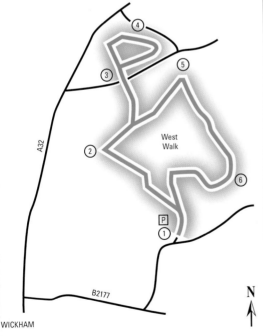

ROUTE 23
WEST WALK (HAMPSHIRE)

ROUTE INSTRUCTIONS:
The route is well signposted.

1. From the car park take the left-hand fork, signposted with a red bike on a green square. On a gentle descent take the first broad track to the left (signposted).

2. At a five-way junction of tracks at the bottom of the hill turn right (signposted) then shortly first left (this is the start of the side loop, shaped like a balloon with a string).

3. Descend, climb, go through the car park, cross the road (with care) and continue straight ahead through the barrier.

4. At the crossroads at the bottom turn right and follow the broad gravel track round to the right to complete the loop (the balloon!). Turn left (along the string!), recross the road (take care) and go straight ahead.

5. At the T-junction turn left to rejoin the main loop, then at a crossroads after $1/2$ mile turn right (signposted).

6. On a long, steady climb keep an eye out for a signpost directing you sharply right by a wooden bench. Descend back to the start.

BACKGROUND AND PLACES OF INTEREST

CENTURION WAY, CHICHESTER
(On the north side of Chichester)

A short section of railway path between Chichester and Mid Lavant passing some extraordinary metal sculptures of Roman centurions and 'surveyors'. The route passes through woodland and arable land with a profusion of wildflowers along the verges. The name 'Centurion Way' was suggested by a local schoolboy and is based on the fact that the path crosses the course of a Roman road. It is hoped that in the future the path will be extended north beyond Lavant. At its southern end the path meets the South Coast Cycle Route, part of Sustrans' National Cycle Network, which as National Route 2 will eventually run along the length of the South Coast from Kent to Cornwall!

History of the Railway

The Chichester to Midhurst Railway was opened in 1881 to improve access to London. The line included three tunnels and eight stations, the most notable of the latter being Singleton, due to its proximity to Goodwood racecourse. The railway's decline started with the withdrawal of passenger services in 1935 and the line north of Lavant was closed completely in 1957. The section between Lavant and Chichester was subsequently used for freight until 1991. In 1994 the County Council purchased the railway line and with investment and help from English Partnerships, Chichester District Council and Tarmac Quarry Products the old railway line was converted to recreational use.

Right: Chichester Cathedral.
The South East England Tourist Board

Below: The curious metal sculpture at the start of the Centurion Way.

Starting Points and Parking: 1. There is a car park at the northern end of the railway path, in Mid Lavant. Coming from the north, turn left off the A286 in Mid Lavant, just before the wooden-spired church, on to St Nicholas Road. Follow the road to the left then turn right on to Springfield Close and right again on to Churchmead Close, now following signs for 'Chichester Cycle Route'. The car park is along on the left, the trail goes beneath the railway bridge.

2. The southern end of the path is on the west side of Chichester near the College of Technology. Follow Westgate from the centre of Chichester, straight over a roundabout past the Swan PH signposted '7.5 ton weight limit'. Continue following Westgate until just before the railway lines — bear right on to a tarmac path then shortly turn left on to the Centurion Way.

Distance: 3 miles one way, 6 miles return.

Map/Leaflet: Ordnance Survey Landranger Sheet 197. A simple, A4 leaflet about the Centurion Way is available from West Sussex County Council, Local Transport Planning Section, County Surveyor and Engineer's Dept, Chichester, West Sussex PO19 1RH (Tel: 01243 777353).

Hills: There are no hills.

Surface: Good quality gravel track.

Roads and Road Crossings: None on the route. You will need to use roads if you are starting from/visiting the centre of Chichester.

Refreshments: Earl of March PH in Mid Lavant; lots of choice in Chichester.

ROUTE INSTRUCTIONS:
Once you have found the start of the route, whether in Chichester or Mid Lavant, there is no need for instructions: follow the railway path for 3 miles until it stops!

Right: Chichester Harbour.
The South East England Tourist Board

Top Right: Market Square, Chichester..
The South East England Tourist Board

Top Centre: The Roman road surveyors!

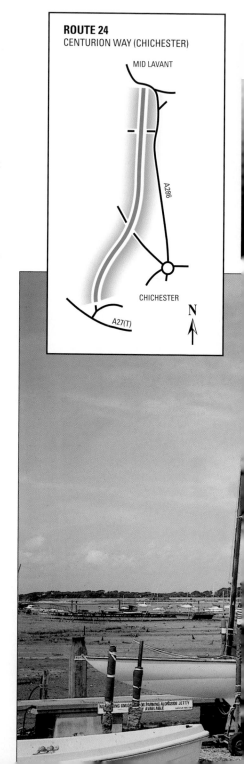

ROUTE 24
CENTURION WAY (CHICHESTER)

MID LAVANT

A286

CHICHESTER

A27(T)

N

HOUGHTON FOREST, ARUNDEL

(4 miles north of Arundel)

There are several large Forestry Commission holdings along the South Downs Way between Petersfield and Arundel, two of which have waymarked trails in them. The first of these is in Queen Elizabeth Park (described in Route 20) which also has the attraction of a well-laid-out Visitor Centre. The ride described here has an outdoor café in a large car park rather than a Visitor Centre but the waymarked ride is easier and there are many options for extending the route and taking in more forest tracks or sections of the South Downs Way. There is plenty else of interest nearby: the old Roman Road of Stane Street passes right by the Roman Villa at Bignor (65 rooms, splendid mosaics) on its way from Chichester to London; Arundel Castle with its Toy and Military Museum stands glorious and intact just 3 miles south of Houghton Forest; Amberley Castle is considerably less intact but set in a delightful village near the River Arun and a little further afield are Petworth Deer Park and Chichester cathedral.

BACKGROUND AND PLACES OF INTEREST

Arundel Castle
The castle was completed after the Norman Conquest to defend the Arun Valley, one of six regions of Sussex in Norman times. The castle is the ancestral home of the Dukes of Norfolk and is flanked by a fine 19th-century cathedral.

This Spread: Arundel Castle across the River Arun. *The South East England Tourist Board*

Inset: Keep an eye out for bike signs — some are easy to miss.

Starting Point and Parking: The Whiteways car park just off the roundabout at the junction of the A29, A284 and B2139 to the north of Arundel.

Distance: 4-mile circuit.

Map: Ordnance Survey Landranger Sheet 197.

Hills: There is one hill of 170ft in the first half of the ride.

Surface: Stone and gravel forestry tracks.

Roads and Road Crossings: None.

Refreshments: Tea wagon in the car park.

ROUTE INSTRUCTIONS:
The route is generally well signposted.

1. The trail starts opposite the entrance to the car park. Follow the main track directly away from the road, signposted 'Public Bridleway to Bike Trail'.

2. Follow the signs showing a white bike on a green background. At a major fork of tracks on the descent bear left.

3. Short descent, long steady climb. Easy to miss! Keep an eye out for a bike sign indicating a track to the right. (This is opposite a two-way 'Public Bridleway' signpost.) Shortly turn right again at the crossroads of tracks.

4. At the T-junction at the bottom of the descent turn right and follow this track back to the car park.

Right: Is this sign really 2000 years old?

Far Right: Mosaic at Bignor Roman Villa.
The South East England Tourist Board.

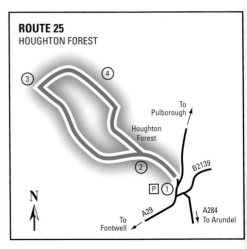

ROUTE 25
HOUGHTON FOREST

THE SOUTH DOWNS RIDGE FROM KITHURST HILL
(2 miles southwest of Storrington)

The South Downs Way is a long-distance bridleway that stretches for 100 miles from Winchester to Eastbourne. It follows the line of chalk hills that rise to over 800ft between the Sussex Weald and the English Channel. In its entirety it would be a tough challenge in the summer months for fit mountain bikers. For those who would prefer not to face lung-bursting 600ft climbs but would nevertheless like to enjoy the wonderful views from the ridge and the pleasure of riding along the broad, chalk and flint tracks there are several short 3-4-mile sections which can be easily accessed by road. In addition to the ride described below, the other sections of the South Downs Way worth considering for similar rides are: Chanctonbury Ring from the minor road between Steyning and Sompting; Firle Beacon from West Firle and Ditchling Beacon north of Brighton.

BACKGROUND AND PLACES OF INTEREST

Amberley
This attractive village has a ruined castle dating back to the 14th century built for the Bishops of Chichester, a Norman church and several thatched cottages. There is a Museum of Local Industry in the former chalk quarry.

Starting Point and Parking: The Kithurst Hill car park (Grid Reference 070124) at the top of the minor road leading up from the B2139 between Storrington and Amberley. As you head west from Storrington towards Amberley, the lane you need to take is the first on the left after the end of the restricted speed limit. Climb to the car park right at the top.

Distance: 1. West — 1 mile one way, 2 miles return. 2. East — 2½ miles one way, 5 miles return.

Map: Ordnance Survey Landranger Sheets 197 and 198.

Hills: A gentle 100ft climb to the trig point to the west (Rackham Hill). A slightly steeper 130ft climb to the east on to Kithurst Hill.

Surface: Stone, chalk and flint track, likely to be muddy in winter.

Roads and Road Crossings: None.

Refreshments: None on route, and a very steep descent down to either Amberley (to the west) or Washington (to the east) should you follow the South Downs Way to these villages.

ROUTE INSTRUCTIONS:
From the Kithurst Hill car park go through the barrier on to the South Downs Way. There are two possible rides:

1. Turn right (west) for 1 mile. Follow the South Downs Way, taking the right-hand fork soon after a small woodland section, going as far as the trig point (up in the field at the end of the fairly flat section). Beyond the trig point there is a 600ft descent to Amberley in the valley of the River Arun which would be great fun going down on a mountain bike but not so much fun coming back up!

2. Turn left (east) for 2½ miles. Climb, descend then climb again. It is suggested you go beyond the barn and stop at the brow of the hill at the junction of tracks by a signpost which says 'Safe Road Crossing — South Downs Way'. Beyond here there is a steep descent to Washington.
NB: Don't be tempted to use the B2139 to make this into a circular ride — it is a fast and busy road unsuitable for quiet recreational cycling.

ROUTE 26
KITHURST HILL (SOUTH DOWNS WAY)

STORRINGTON

A283

B2139

Rackham
Hill

①

Kithurst
Hill

②

Barnsfarm
Hill

N

P
Start Point

South Downs Way

Far Left: One of the few easy sections of the
South Downs Way.

Above: Broad chalk track through rolling
downland.

Left: Potter at work, Amberley Museum.
The South East England Tourist Board

THE DOWNS LINK FROM BRAMBER TO OLD SHOREHAM

(5 miles east of Worthing)

Bramber is a very attractive village at the foot of the South Downs, located on the banks of the tidal River Adur, one of only three rivers that flow south from the Weald to cut a course through the chalk hills of the South Downs. The ride runs south from Bramber alongside the river to Old Shoreham where there is a

Bottom: Along the Downs Link, near Old Shoreham.

Inset: Refreshment shop in Bramber.

choice of refreshment stops. There is plenty of wildlife to see along the river and fine views of Lancing College from the southern end of the ride.

NB: There is one difficult road crossing near the start of the ride. Please take extreme care crossing the A283 just south of Bramber.

BACKGROUND AND PLACES OF INTEREST

The Downs Link

The Downs Link bridleway links the North Downs Way at St Martha's Hill near Guildford with the South Downs Way south of Steyning and follows the course of an old railway line for much of its 30-mile length. The railway fell victim to the Beeching axe in 1966.

Bramber Castle

This National Trust property consists of the ruins of a Norman fortress built in 1083. The Civil War resulted in its destruction by Parliamentarians.

Old Shoreham

The village was stranded a mile inland when the harbour silted up in the 11th century so 'New' Shoreham was built as the new port.

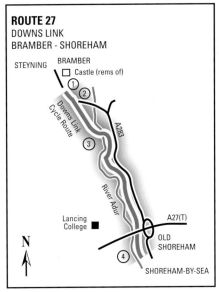

ROUTE 27
DOWNS LINK
BRAMBER - SHOREHAM

STEYNING BRAMBER
☐ Castle (rems of)

①
②

Downs Link
Cycle Route

A283

③

River Adur

Lancing
College ■

A27(T)

OLD
SHOREHAM

④

N
↑

SHOREHAM-BY-SEA

Refreshments: Ye Bramber Castle Hotel, Bramber; Amsterdam PH, Red Lion Inn, Old Shoreham.

ROUTE INSTRUCTIONS:
The route is signposted with 'Downs Link' signs.

1. Exit the car park in the centre of Bramber and turn right on the road as far as the roundabout. There is a 'Downs Link' sign immediately before the roundabout directing you on to a track running parallel with the southbound A283.

2. Take extreme care crossing the A283 to the other side. Wait patiently until you have gauged the speed of the traffic and there is a clear gap for you to cross.

3. At the T-junction of tracks turn left, signposted 'South Downs Way. Eastbourne'. Cross the river bridge then turn right, signposted 'Coastal Link'.

4. Follow the track alongside the river for 3 miles. It is suggested you go as far as the Amsterdam PH/Red Lion Inn in Old Shoreham then return. (Beyond this point the trail soon peters out.)

Starting Point and Parking: The car park in Bramber, a village signposted off the A283 roundabout at the south end of the Steyning bypass. The ride itself starts at the roundabout with the A283 (there is a 'Downs Link' sign at the northeast corner of the roundabout).

Distance: 4 miles one way, 8 miles return.

Map: Ordnance Survey Landranger Sheet 198.

Hills: There are no hills.

Surface: Good quality gravel tracks. A short section close to the river is slightly rougher.

Roads and Road Crossings: Extreme care should be taken crossing the A283 south of Bramber near the start of the ride. Take plenty of time to gauge the speed of the traffic before crossing, particularly if you are with young children. If you wish to miss this bit out altogether you could start from the church in Old Shoreham and ride north as far as the A283 before turning around.

Above Left: Where did this fly in from?

DEVIL'S DYKE RAILWAY TRAIL FROM HANGLETON, HOVE
(2 miles north of Hove)

This short trail climbs along the course of an old railway line from the outskirts of Hove right up on to the South Downs ridge with magnificent views northwards across the Sussex Weald. It would be possible to make this into a longer ride by turning left along the South Downs Way as far as the masts on Truleigh Hill, although this would involve using some rougher sections of bridleway and quite a few ups and downs! It is worth waiting for a day with good visibility to do this ride as the views from the top are spectacular.

BACKGROUND AND PLACES OF INTEREST

History of the Line

The Dyke Railway opened in 1887 and ran from Aldrington Halt for 3½ miles up to the Devil's Dyke station at an almost continuous gradient of 1 in 40. It was never a very profitable route and finally closed in 1938. The line served the Brighton & Hove Golf Club where a halt was constructed in 1891. In 1895 a bell was installed between the golf clubhouse and the Dyke station which would sound in the golf club bar on the departure of a train from the terminus, allowing members time to drink up in the bar and still catch their train home!

Devil's Dyke

It is said that this was created by the Devil in an attempt to flood the many Wealden churches. It is in fact a natural formation in the chalk hillside rising over 300ft on either side. The Dyke viewpoint was the site of a massive hillfort dating back to the Iron Age and one of the largest of its kind on the South Downs. The highest point is marked by a triangulation pillar.

This Spread: Brighton's West Pier.

Inset: The Devil Dyke trail climbs up from the coast at Hove.

Starting Point and Parking: The trail starts in the suburb of Hangleton, on the northern outskirts of Hove (Grid Reference 270076). There is a car park at the start of the trail in Hangleton between the Countryman PH and the row of shops. These are located a short distance up the hill from St Helen's church.

Distance: 3 miles one way, 6 miles return.

Map: Ordnance Survey Landranger Sheet 198.

Hills: There is a steady 450ft climb from the start up to the viewpoint/trig point at Devil's Dyke PH. So it is a lot quicker coming back than going up!

Surface: Good quality track.

Above: Devil's Dyke.

Right: The clocktower on Palace Pier.

Roads and Road Crossings: A section of road is used for just over a mile from the end of the railway path up to the viewpoint. For much of its length there is a parallel track alongside which varies in quality.

Refreshments: Devil's Dyke PH at the top.

ROUTE INSTRUCTIONS:
1. Climb steadily from the Hangleton car park. Cross the bridge over the A27.

2. Go past the golf course. When you are parallel with the golf clubhouse (to your right) turn left on to a continuation of the railway path.

3. At the road either turn left on tarmac or cross the road and turn left on a track parallel with the road. (Remember this point for the return trip.)

4. Where the road swings right, bear left to continue climbing towards Devil's Dyke.

5. After reaching the top you may wish simply to return. As an option to make the ride longer you could follow the South Downs Way west as far as Truleigh masts. This is a further 6-mile round trip on a track (at times rough) which undulates between 500ft and 700ft above sea level, with wonderful views of the Weald.

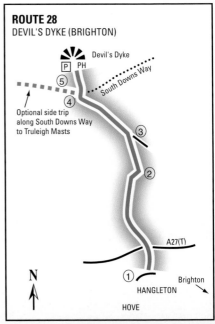

ROUTE 28
DEVIL'S DYKE (BRIGHTON)

THE
PALACE PIER
PALACE PIER
We Apologise
NO DOGS
NO BICYCLES
NO
CAUTION
ATTRACTIONS
FREE
FUN
FREE
Admission
FREE
Deck Chairs
FREE
Entertainmen
Free Family Entertainment

BEDGEBURY FOREST, KENT
(4 miles southwest of Cranbrook, Kent)

This is the only waymarked forestry route in Kent and probably the hardest thing about it is finding the start! It lies down an unmarked minor road (see 'Starting Point and Parking', below). Bedgebury Forest is mixed woodland and amongst the fir and conifers you will find sweet chestnut, birch, oak and sycamore, not to mention bright yellow ragwort, purple willow-herb and foxgloves. The forest lies adjacent to Bedgebury Pinetum which contains a magnificent collection of rare trees and flowering shrubs. There is a lovely picnic spot by the lakes you pass along the route.

BACKGROUND AND PLACES OF INTEREST

Bedgebury Pinetum
The Pinetum holds Europe's foremost collection of conifers. Azaleas and rhododendrons add colour.

Right: The Bedgebury Pinetum.

Below: Nearby Bewl Water, where there is also a cycle trail.

Left: Smile —
there's no
traffic!

Starting Point and Parking: The start of the cycle trail in Bedgebury Forest lies at the end of a minor road running west from the A229 Cranbrook-Hawkhurst road. This unsigned minor road is difficult to find! Coming south from Cranbrook towards Hawkhurst, ¾ mile after passing the B2085 to Goudhurst on the right, it is the first proper road to the right. (The turn off the A229 is located at Grid Reference 759335.) Follow the minor road to its end. There is parking just after the end of the tarmac.

Distance: 5-mile circuit.

Map: Ordnance Survey Landranger Sheet 188.

Hills: There are several gentle hills.

Surface: Good quality gravel tracks.

Roads and Road Crossings: There are no roads or road crossings.

Refreshments: The Old Trout PH, Flimwell, is just off the route.

ROUTE INSTRUCTIONS:
The route is well signposted.

1. From the car park on the eastern edge of the forest take the left-hand fork signposted 'Forest Cycle Trail. 5 miles'. After ½ mile, at the bike signpost, turn right off the main stone track on to a narrower, rougher track. At the first T-junction turn right, at the second T-junction (with a wide stone track) turn left.

2. Go past a lake. Climb then descend. At the next T-junction, with wooden barns to the left, turn right (or for the Old Trout PH in Flimwell turn left then left again alongside the A21).

3. Go past a second barn (with corrugated iron roof). At the T-junction after 1 mile turn right (or to visit the Pinetum turn left).

4. At a point after ½ mile where a track turns off to the left you have a choice of continuing straight ahead back to the start (signposted 'Short Cut') or of taking this left turn (signposted 'Sugar Loaf Hill') and following the waymarked route which takes a slightly longer course to return to the start.

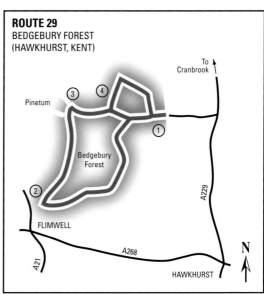

ROUTE 29
BEDGEBURY FOREST
(HAWKHURST, KENT)

🚲 **ROUTE 30**

KING'S WOOD AND CHILHAM, KENT
(6 miles north of Ashford)

Kent has several Forestry Commission holdings where there are enough broad stone tracks to make an enjoyable circuit, although only Bedgebury Forest has a signposted route (see Route 29). In addition to the circuit within the wood itself, this ride offers you a chance to follow the ancient North Downs Way (used by pilgrims on their way to

Right: Forest road in King's Wood.

Inset: The tea room at Chilham.

Below: Even bikes need a rest!

Canterbury) and to drop down into the delightful village of Chilham with its lovely buildings, fine choice of pubs and a tearoom.

BACKGROUND AND PLACES OF INTEREST

King's Wood

As an ancient woodland King's Wood is home to a great diversity of wildflowers including typical woodland species such as wood sorrel, bluebells and foxgloves. There are also some more unusual species such as columbine, common spotted orchid and deadly nightshade. King's Wood is a working forest where timber harvesting is an ongoing activity. You will see many areas of sweet chestnut coppice where the tree is cut in 15-year cycles to enable new shoots to grow from the stump. This traditional form of harvesting wood benefits the fauna and flora of the woodland and is used to benefit the rural economy by producing timber for fencing and paper.

Starting Point and Parking: From the roundabout at the junction of the A252 and A251 at Challock (north of Ashford) follow the A251 south towards Ashford for ¾ mile then take the first road to the left, signposted 'Wye'. The car park is ½ mile along here on the left.

Distance: Short route — 6 miles. Full route — 12 miles.

Map: Ordnance Survey Landranger Sheet 189.

Hills: There are several gentle hills on the forestry circuit. There is a steep 300ft hill if you choose to do the side trip to Chilham.

Surface: Good quality gravel tracks in the forest. The North Downs Way is a bit rougher and likely to become muddy in winter or after prolonged rain.

Roads and Road Crossings: There is a short section on a minor road at the start and finish of the ride. If you choose to go down into Chilham there is a 1-mile section on a very minor no through road.

Refreshments: Tearoom and pubs in Chilham.

ROUTE INSTRUCTIONS:
1. Exit the car park and turn right along the road for ½ mile. Turn right into the wood just before this minor road joins the A251. The entrance is located by a low wooden post just before the locked gates on the right. Follow the right-hand one of the two broad stone tracks ahead.

2. Steady descent. Ignore turnings to right and left and go straight ahead at the crossroads. There are three downhills and three uphills. At the T-junction at the top of the third climb (a steep climb where you will probably have to push) you will come to a wooden post with red, yellow and blue arrows on it. At this point you have a choice:
(a). Short route. Turn right signposted 'North Downs Way' (red arrow). Rejoin at instruction No 6 'Continue straight ahead...'

(b). Full route with side trip to Chilham. (This involves a steep descent and a steep climb to return to this point.) Turn left along the North Downs Way, passing a stone marker down to your left with distances to Farnham and Dover on it.

3. At a T-junction by a wooden bridlegate adjoining a metal field gate turn right, signposted 'North Downs Way' (remember this point for the return). Steep descent (take care). Join the minor lane and continue downhill in the same direction.

4. After 1 mile, on a sharp right-hand bend turn left uphill on School Hill to arrive at the square in Chilham. Explore the delights of the village (lovely old buildings, food and drink) and retrace your steps, leaving the square via School Hill and turning right at the T-junction at the bottom.

5. Climb back up the outward route and follow the North Downs Way. After 1 mile you will pass the stone 'Farnham/Canterbury' milepost at the point where the outward route joined the North Downs Way.

6. Continue straight ahead for a further mile and take the next major, broad grass and stone track to the right, signposted with a red dot and blue arrow. There is a short section of rough track. At the T-junction with a smoother track turn left.

7. At the next T-junction bear left then at the road turn right to return to the start.

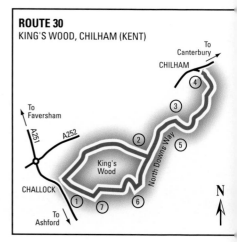

ROUTE 30
KING'S WOOD, CHILHAM (KENT)

Above: Kent Oast Houses near Chilham.

Left: Stopping for a break on a tour of Southern England.

A. THE FIRST *CYCLING WITHOUT TRAFFIC: SOUTHEAST*

The 30 routes below are described more fully in the first *Cycling Without Traffic: Southeast*, available from all good bookshops.

1. A circuit of Grafham Water, west of Cambridge.
2. The Grand Union Canal through Milton Keynes.
3. Priory Country Park and the Willington Countryway, Bedford.
4. The Flitch Way from Braintree to Little Dunmow.
5. The Ridgeway near Watlington.
6. The Grand Union Canal from London | to Tring.
7. The Nicky Line from Harpenden to Hemel Hempstead.
8. The Ayot Greenway from Wheathampstead to Welwyn Garden City.
9. The Albanway from St Albans to Hatfield.
10. The Cole Greenway, west of Hertford.
11. Regent's Canal and the Lee Navigation in East London.
12. A circuit in Epping Forest.
13. The Kennet & Avon Canal towpath near Thatcham.
14. Windsor Great Park.
15. The Basingstoke Canal from Weybridge to Odiham.
16. The Thames Towpath between Putney Bridge and Weybridge.
17. Wimbledon Common, Putney Heath and Richmond Park.
18. The Test Way, south from Stockbridge.
19. The Meon Valley Trail from West Meon to Wickham.
20. The Downs Link from Cranleigh to Henfield.
21. The Worth Way, west of East Grinstead.
22. The Forest Way, East Grinstead to Groombridge.
23. The South Downs Way near Chanctonbury Ring.
24. The South Downs Way near Ditchling Beacon.
25. The South Downs Way near Firle Beacon.
26. Friston Forest, west of Eastbourne.
27. The Cuckoo Trail from Polegate to Heathfield.
28. A circuit of Bewl Water, near Tunbridge Wells.
29. The North Downs Way from Charing to Maidstone.
30. The Royal Military Canal, west of Hythe.

B. OTHER ROUTES IN BRIEF

Below is a further list of traffic-free routes in the region that we simply did not have the space to include in the main section. The brief description given for each of these routes should enable you to find the start of the trail and know what sort of ride you are likely to enjoy.

1. The Slough Arm of the Grand Union Canal
A 5-mile ride along a canal towpath starting ½ mile north of Slough railway station on the B416 (Grid Reference 979807) and running east to join the Grand Union Canal near Yiewsley (Grid Reference 056809).

2. Flitch Way
A railway path to the west of Braintree in Essex. The Braintree to Little Dunmow section is covered in the first *Cycling Without Traffic: Southeast*. However, you can also ride another section, located to the west of Great Dunmow. The best starting point is at the old station in Takeley (Grid Reference 564211), just south of the A120. You can follow the Flitch Way for 3 miles in either direction.

3. The Kennet & Avon Canal
The canal towpath can be followed from Theale (Grid Reference 647706) into the centre of Reading, where it joins the River Thames.

4. Parkland Walk, Highgate and Finsbury Park, North London
A short 2½-mile railway path from Holmesdale Road, Highgate (near the junction of Archway Road and Shepherd's Hill) to Finsbury Park, where you can complete a circuit of the park.

5. Canterbury University to Whitstable
A mixture of newly-built woodland path and railway path starting northwest of Canterbury near the university and Kent College (Grid Reference 130599) and running north for 4 miles to South Street, south of Whitstable (Grid Reference 124650).

6. Yarmouth to Freshwater on the Isle of Wight
A short 2½-mile railway path from Yarmouth, at the western end of the Isle of Wight, south to Freshwater. If you catch the ferry from

Lymington to Yarmouth this is a good connection to the Tennyson Trail (Route 21, page 70).

7. Shanklin-Wroxall
Another 2½-mile railway path on the Isle of Wight, this time at the eastern end of the island. The ride starts from just west of Shanklin railway station (Grid Reference 577817) by the entrance to the holiday park and runs southwest to the church in Wroxall.

8. Brighton & Hove Seafront Cycle Route
A 2½-mile route along the seafront on a segregated cycle path from Hove Lagoon (Grid Reference 271045) to Brighton's Palace Pier (Grid Reference 314038).

C. LONG-DISTANCE TRAILS IN THE SOUTHEAST

1. THE RIDGEWAY/ICKNIELD WAY
A long-distance trail open to cyclists from West Kennet (near Avebury) to Princes Risborough. A 6-mile stretch is described in Route 12. The longest rideable section runs west from the Thames at Streatley up on to the Berkshire Downs, across the Lambourn Downs and past Swindon to near Marlborough, a distance of 35 miles. The route is well signposted and immense improvements have been made in the last few years to repair the deep ruts caused by the four-wheel-drive vehicles which have a right to use the track. Mountain bikes are recommended if you intend to do the whole route.

2. THE NORTH DOWNS WAY
The North Downs Way is an official long-distance footpath which means that it is much better signposted and maintained than any ordinary right of way and therefore easier to follow. However, its status alternates between footpath, bridleway and byway and you are NOT allowed to cycle on it where it is a footpath. A 3-mile section north of Reigate is described in Route 18. There is a long stretch between Dorking and Guildford which has bridleway status, but apart from these two sections, you will have to look carefully at an Ordnance Survey map to see whether you are allowed to cycle along the North Downs Way.

Left: Or would you rather be in a supermarket?

3. THE SOUTH DOWNS WAY

By contrast with the North Downs Way, the South Downs Way is a bridleway along its entire length and would make a good challenge for fit cyclists on mountain bikes. It runs for 100 miles from Winchester to Eastbourne with many thousands of feet of climbing. There are, however, several easier, short sections where you can start at a car park at the top of the ridge and explore the trail for a short distance either side of the starting point, maintaining height and enjoying magnificent views out to the English Channel and down into the Sussex Weald. A 3½-mile section southwest of Storrington is described in Route 26. Three other similar sections can be recommended: near Chanctonbury Ring, Firle Beacon and Ditchling Beacon (these are covered in the first *Cycling Without Traffic: Southeast*).

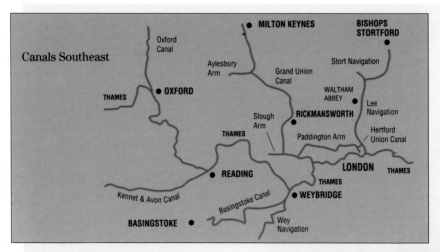

Canals Southeast

D. CANAL TOWPATHS AND REGIONAL WATERWAYS BOARDS

The theory is that there are 2,000 miles of towpaths in England and Wales, offering flat, vehicle-free cycling. The reality is that only a fraction of the towpath network is suitable for cycling; the rest is too narrow, overgrown, muddy and rough. There is obviously much room for improvement and certain waterways boards, in conjunction with local authorities and the Countryside Commission, have made immense progress in improving towpaths for all user groups.

The southeast of the country is well served, with long stretches of good-quality towpaths alongside all the waterways which radiate from London. However, even the areas which have a reasonable surface are often busy with anglers and walkers, so cycle slowly, use your bell and give way to other towpath users. (Follow the Waterways Code for Cyclists, opposite.)

Four rides in the book use stretches of canal towpath: Route 5 runs right through Oxford on a mixture of the Thames Path and the Oxford Canal; Routes 9 and 11 explore the Lee & Stort Navigation and the plethora of excellent tracks in the Lee Valley, north of London; Route 15 follows the Wey Navigation south from its junction with the Thames at Weybridge to the pub at Pyrford Lock.

The best cycling escape routes from London are along the watercourses of the River Thames and the canals: the Grand Union Canal starts near Paddington and runs west to Hayes then north through Uxbridge to Rickmansworth and Watford; the Thames itself can be followed from Putney Bridge southwest to Weybridge; from Weybridge it is possible to link via the Wey Navigation (see Route 15) to the Basingstoke Canal which finishes near Odiham in deepest Hampshire; to the northeast, the Lee Valley offers an exit to Waltham Abbey, Ware and Hertford; to the east, the National Cycle Network is building a route close to the Thames from Greenwich to Erith.

For the rest of the canal network please refer to the map and to the addresses and phone numbers of the local waterways board covering your area. There is no overall guideline about cycling on towpaths: some authorities issue a permit and charge for it, others issue a free permit; some have opened up the whole towpath to cyclists, others allow cycling only on certain sections. The most up-to-date information can be obtained from your local waterways board.

The addresses and phone numbers are as follows:

- **Oxford Canal and Grand Union Canal North**
  British Waterways, The Stop House, Braunston, Northamptonshire NN11 7JQ (Tel: 01788 890666).

- **Grand Union Canal South**
  British Waterways, Marsworth Junction, Watery Lane, Marsworth, Tring, Hertfordshire HP23 4LZ (Tel: 020 7286 6101).

- **Kennet & Avon Canal**
  British Waterways, Bath Road, Devizes, Wiltshire SN10 1HB (Tel: 01380 722859).

- **Basingstoke Canal**
  Basingstoke Canal Authority, Ash Lock Depot, Government Road, Aldershot, Hampshire GU11 2PS (Tel: 01252 370073).

- **River Wey & Godalming Navigation Office,**
  National Trust, Dapdune Wharf, Wharf Road, Guildford, Surrey GU1 4RR (Tel: 01483 561389).

THE WATERWAYS CODE FOR CYCLISTS

1. Access paths can be steep and slippery — join the towing path with care.

2. Always give way to other people on the towing path and warn them of your approach, A 'hello' and 'thank you' mean a lot. Be prepared to dismount if the path is busy with pedestrians or anglers.

3. You must dismount and push your cycle if the path narrows, or passes beneath a low bridge or alongside a lock.

4. Ride at a gentle pace, in single file, and do not bunch.

5. Never race — you have water on one side of you.

6. Watch out when passing moored boats — there may be mooring spikes concealed on the path.

7. Take particular care on wet or uneven surfaces, and don't worsen them by skidding.

8. Never cycle along towing paths in the dark.

9. Towing paths are not generally suitable for organised cycling events, but the local Waterways Manager may give permission.

10. If you encounter a dangerous hazard, please notify the Waterways Manager at the regional office.

Please remember you are responsible for your own and others' safety! You are only allowed to cycle on towing paths if you follow this code.

Centre Left: Excellent towpath — as they all should be!

Bottom Left: The canal network was mainly built from 1760-1830.

E. FORESTRY COMMISSION LAND

The Forestry Commission owns many thousands of acres of land in the area covered by this book and has, by and large, adopted an enlightened approach to cycling in its woodlands. The broad rule of thumb is that you are allowed to ride on the hard, stone-based forestry roads which provide excellent opportunities for safe, family cycling. You are NOT allowed to cycle in the woodland away from these hard tracks and should pay attention to any signs which may indicate a temporary or permanent restriction on cycling (normally on walkers' trails or where forestry operations are in progress).

In some places, the forestry authorities have even waymarked a trail for cyclists. However, open access is not universally the case, and in some woodlands you are only allowed on tracks where there is a statutory right of way, namely bridleways and byways.

This may all sound a little confusing, but the Forestry Commission is extremely helpful and normally has good reasons for restricting access. The forests are working environments where heavy machinery is often being used to fell or plant trees and whenever work is in progress there will be restrictions on recreational use.

A phone call or a letter to your local Forest Enterprise office should clarify the situation (addresses and phone numbers are listed below). In order to simplify matters as much as possible, forestry areas have been divided into two categories:

(A) sites where a trail has been waymarked for cyclists;
(B) sites where there is an open access policy (except for walkers' trails).

The best maps to use for exploring Forestry Commission woodland are the most up-to-date Ordnance Survey Explorer maps, scale 1:25,000, which tend to be reasonably accurate. Some woodlands are covered by leaflets produced by the Forest Enterprise offices, which are listed below.

PLEASE NOTE: It must be stressed that there are many different user groups enjoying the woodlands, so courtesy and consideration should be shown at all times to walkers and horse riders. The fact that a bike can travel faster than a pedestrian does not give you any priority; indeed, priority normally lies with the walker or the horse rider. Use a bell to give warning of your presence and say thank you to people who step aside for you.

(A) FORESTRY WITH WAYMARKED CYCLE TRAILS

There are eight waymarked trails on Forestry Commission land in the area covered by the book:
1. Wendover Woods, northeast of Wendover (Route 6, page 38).
2. Aston Hill Woods, northeast of Wendover (tough and steep mountain biking).
3. Alice Holt Forest, southwest of Farnham (Route 19, page 66).
4. West Walk, northwest of Fareham (Route 23, page 78).
5. Queen Elizabeth Country Park, south of Petersfield (Route 20, page 68).
6. Houghton Forest, northwest of Arundel (Route 25, page 84).
7. Friston Forest, west of Eastbourne (covered in the first *Cycling Without Traffic: Southeast*).
8. Bedgebury, southwest of Cranbrook (Route 29, page 96).

(B) OTHER FORESTRY AREAS

In addition to the waymarked forestry trails listed above there are many small Forest Enterprise holdings throughout the southeast of England where it would be possible to devise your own short routes on hard forestry roads. These are concentrated:

1. Between Ashford and Canterbury.
2. Between Petersfield and Arundel.
3. To the north of Fleet.

The best publication showing all these holdings is a 48-page A4 booklet called *Ramblers' Atlas of Public Forests* published by the Ramblers' Association. It is available free by sending a large (A4) stamped addressed envelope with 52p of stamps to the Ramblers' Association, 1/5 Wandsworth Road, London SW8 2XX. This together with

Right: You can progress from railway paths to byways and bridleways.

the appropriate Ordnance Survey Landranger (1:50,000) or Explorer (1:25,000) map will allow you to see your options and plan your routes.

It is also worth contacting the following Forest Enterprise District Offices for further information:

- **South East England Forest District,** Bucks Horn Oak, Farnham, Surrey GU10 4LS (Tel: 01420 23666).

- **East Anglia Forest District, Santon** Downham, Brandon, Suffolk IP27 0TJ (Tel: 01842 810271).

F. SUSTRANS' NATIONAL CYCLE NETWORK

The National Cycle Network is a linked series of traffic-free paths and traffic-calmed roads being developed right across the United Kingdom, linking town centres and the countryside. The Millennium Routes (2,500 miles) are open in 2000 and a further 5,500 miles will open by 2005.

In the region covered by this book there are four long sections of the National Cycle Network that are open in 2000:

Below: See the countryside from your saddle.

1. London to Oxford (the Thames Valley Cycle Route). The route largely follows the Thames riverside path from Putney Bridge to Weybridge (ideal family cycling). There are also enjoyable traffic-free sections through Reading (see Route 13) and alongside the Thames in Oxford (see Route 5).

2. London to Eastbourne. The route starts at the Millennium Dome in London and goes south via what is known as the Waterlink Way running down through Deptford, Catford and Lewisham towards Croydon and Redhill. After crossing the High Weald to East Grinstead, the route soon joins the popular Cuckoo Trail (ideal family cycling) from Heathfield down to Polegate.

3. London to Dover. To the east of the Dome and the Thames Barrier the National Cycle Network continues along the Thames estuary as far as Gravesend where it heads inland through Kent on to Canterbury and Dover.

4. Dover to Eastbourne. Completing the London-Dover-Eastbourne triangle, this coastal route passes through Folkestone and Hastings with a newly built traffic-free section between Rye and Camber.

LOCAL AUTHORITY LEAFLETS

Local authorities often produce cycling leaflets, such as town maps showing urban cycle networks or leaflets describing recreational routes in the countryside. However, when trying to obtain these leaflets, do not expect any logic or consistency: not only does the quantity and quality of leaflets vary from one authority to the next but each authority seems to have a different name for the department in charge of cycling! In addition, some charge for their leaflets and some give them away free. Just to complicate matters further, local authorities are forever reorganising and changing department names; then of course leaflets run out and are not reprinted...

As you can see, it would be very easy to give information that would be out of date almost as soon as this book is published, so instead we are suggesting that you become the detective and find out from your own local authority what cycling leaflets they have produced. Below is a list of the addresses and main telephone numbers of each of the local authorities (County Councils, Metropolitan Councils, Unitary Authorities) in the area covered by this book.

When you call, ask to speak to 'The Cycling Officer' or to someone about recreational or family cycling. You may be put through to one of the following departments: Planning, Highways, Tourism, Transport, Environment, Access & Recreation or the Countryside Section and do not be surprised to be transferred from one department to another! Have a pen and paper handy so that when you do get through to the right person you can note down their name and their direct phone line and the address to which you should send money (if required). They may also be able to help you with the names of people to speak to in the adjoining authorities.

An alternative to this is to contact Sustrans' Information Service, PO Box 21, Bristol BS99 2HA (Tel: 0117 929 0888) or visit its website at www.sustrans.org.uk. For a small handling fee Sustrans should be able to provide you with the leaflets you require.

LOCAL AUTHORITIES' ADDRESSES AND TELEPHONE NUMBERS

Bedfordshire
County Hall, Cauldwell Street,
Bedford MK42 9AP. Tel: 01234 363222.

Bracknell Forest
Civic Offices, Town Square,
Bracknell RG12 1AQ. Tel: 01344 424642.

Brighton & Hove
Kings House, Grand Avenue,
Hove BN3 2LS. Tel: 01273 291000.

Buckinghamshire
County Hall, Aylesbury HP20 1UA.
Tel: 01296 395000.

Cambridgeshire
Shire Hall, Cambridge
CB3 0AP. Tel: 01223 717111.

Essex
County Hall, Chelmsford CM1 1LX.
Tel: 01245 492211.

Hampshire
Mottisfont Court, High Street,
Winchester SO23 8ZF. Tel: 01962 846002.

Hertfordshire
County Hall, Hertford SG13 8DE.
Tel: 01992 555555.

Isle of Wight
County Hall, Newport PO30 1UD.
Tel: 01983 821000.

Kent
County Hall, Sessions House,
Maidstone ME14 1XQ. Tel: 01622 671411.

London Cycling Campaign
3 Stamford Street, London SE1 9NT.
Tel: 020 7928 7220.

There are 33 boroughs in London so rather than give the names and numbers of all of these it is suggested that you join the London Cycling Campaign and find out all the relevant information for the capital.

Luton
Town Hall, Luton LU1 2BQ.
Tel: 01582 746000.

Milton Keynes
Civic Centre, 1 Saxon Gate East, Milton
Keynes MK9 3EJ. Tel: 01908 691691.

Oxfordshire
County Hall, New Road, Oxford, OX1 1ND.
Tel: 01865 815246.

Portsmouth
Civic Offices, Guildhall Square,
Portsmouth PO1 2AL. Tel: 023 9282 2251.

Reading
Civic Centre, Reading RG1 7TD.
Tel: 0118 939 0900.

Slough
Town Hall, Bath Road, Slough SL1 3UQ.
Tel: 01753 552288.

Southampton
Civic Centre, Southampton SO14 7LY.
Tel: 023 8022 3855.

Southend-on-Sea
Civic Centre, Southend-on-Sea SS2 6ER.
Tel: 01702 215000

Suffolk
County Hall, St Helen Court, Ipswich IP4 2JS.
Tel: 01473 583000

Surrey
County Hall, Kingston upon Thames
KT1 2DN. Tel: 020 8541 8800

Sussex (East)
Pelham House, St Andrews Lane,
Lewes BN7 1UN. Tel: 01273 481000

Sussex (West)
County Hall, Chichester PO19 1RQ.
Tel: 01243 777100

West Berkshire
Council Offices, Market Square,
Newbury RG14 5LD. Tel: 01635 42400

Windsor & Maidenhead
Town Hall, St Ives Road, Maidenhead
SL6 1RF. Tel: 01628 796307

TOURIST INFORMATION CENTRES

Another option in your quest for further cycling information is to contact the Tourist Information Centres covering the area in which you are interested. They frequently stock local leaflets and booklets that don't find their way into bookshops or any form of national distribution. Their numbers are listed below.

Brighton	01273 292599
Canterbury	01227 766567
Chelmsford	01245 283400
Chichester	01243 775888
Colchester	01206 282920
Dover	01304 205108
Eastbourne	01323 411400
Guildford	01483 444333
High Wycombe	01494 421892
Horsham	01403 211661
Ipswich	01473 258070
Milton Keynes	01908 558300
Newport (Isle of Wight)	01983 525450
Oxford	01865 726871
Portsmouth	023 9283 8382
Reading	0118 956 6226
Sevenoaks	01732 450305

Cyclists Touring Club (CTC)

Cotterrell House, 69 Meadrow, Godalming, Surrey GU7 3HS.
Tel: 01483 417217.

Britain's largest cycling organisation, promoting recreational and utility cycling. The CTC provides touring and technical advice, legal aid and insurance, and campaigns to improve facilities and opportunities for all cyclists.

Cycle Campaign Network (CCN)

54-57 Allison Street, Digbeth, Birmingham B5 5TH.

National liaison organisation, bringing together information about Britain's many local cycle campaigns. For details of your local cycle campaign group send an SAE to the above address.

This Page: Sorting out family business.

Left: Cycling lets you get away from it all.

Sustrans' Information Service

PO Box 21, Bristol, BS99 2HA .
(Tel: 0117 929 0888).

In 1995 Sustrans won £43 million of lottery funds to help build the 8,000-mile National Cycle Network which will be completed by the year 2005. The Millennium Routes, covering the first 2,500 miles of the Network and open in 2000, include a route stretching from Dover to Inverness. The network uses a mixture of quiet lanes, forestry tracks, canal towpaths, dismantled railways and purpose-built cycleways.

🚲 INDEX